Risotto

GENERAL EDITOR
CHUCK WILLIAMS

RECIPES
KRISTINE KIDD AND OTHER CONTRIBUTORS

PHOTOGRAPHY
ALLAN ROSENBERG

TIME
LIFE
BOOKS

TIME-LIFE BOOKS

Time-Life Books is a division of Time Life Inc.
Time-Life is a trademark of Time Warner Inc. U.S.A.

Time-Life Custom Publishing
Vice President and Publisher: Terry Newell
Vice President of Sales and Marketing: Neil Levin
Director of Financial Operations: J. Brian Birky
Director of Acquisitions: Jennifer L. Pearce

WILLIAMS-SONOMA
Founder and Vice Chairman: Chuck Williams
Associate Book Buyer: Cecilia Michaelis

WELDON OWEN INC.
President: John Owen
Vice President and Publisher: Wendely Harvey
Chief Operating Officer: Larry Partington
Vice President International Sales: Stuart Laurence
Managing Editor: Judith Dunham
Consulting Editor: Norman Kolpas
Copy Editor: Sharon Silva
Design: John Bull, The Book Design Company
Production Director: Stephanie Sherman
Production Consultant: Sarah Lemas
Production Manager: Jen Dalton
Production Editor: Deborah Cowder
Food Photographer: Allan Rosenberg
Additional Photography: Allen V. Lott
Food Stylists: John Phillip Carroll, Peggy Fallon
Prop Stylist: Sandra Griswold
Illustrations: Alice Harth

The Williams-Sonoma Kitchen Library
conceived and produced by Weldon Owen Inc.
814 Montgomery St., San Francisco, CA 94133

In collaboration with Williams-Sonoma
3250 Van Ness Ave., San Francisco, CA 94109

Production by Toppan Printing Co., (HK) Ltd.
Printed in China

A Note on Weights and Measures:
All recipes include customary U.S. and metric measurements. Metric conversions are based on a standard developed for these books and have been rounded off. Actual weights may vary.

A Weldon Owen Production

Copyright © 1998 Weldon Owen Inc.
Reprinted in 1999, 2000

Library of Congress
Cataloging-in-Publication Data:

Kidd, Kristine.
   Risotto / general editor, Chuck Williams ; recipes, Kristine Kidd and other contributors ; photography, Allan Rosenberg.
       p.   cm. — (Williams-Sonoma kitchen library)
   Includes index.
   ISBN 0-7370-2003-2
   1. Cookery (Rice)   2. Risotto.   I. Williams, Chuck.   II. Title.
III. Series.
TX809.R5K531998
641.6'318—dc21   98-3740
                                                                    CIP

Contents

Vegetable Risotto 15

Seafood Risotto 49

Meat & Poultry Risotto 65

Shaped Risotto 93

INTRODUCTION

Risotto has been enjoyed in Italy for centuries but only recently has it gained popularity beyond that country's borders. Nowadays, the rest of us are making up for lost time. The menus of most Italian restaurants feature risottos alongside pastas, and you'll find these wonderful rice dishes on other menus, too, from Mediterranean to Californian.

Why is risotto so popular? An ideal comfort food, it offers the appealing combination of tender, yet chewy rice, creamy sauce, and seasonings, cheese, and other embellishments. And like pasta, risotto presents countless possibilities for variation: the rice can be mixed with nearly any ingredients you like, with delicious results.

That fact is underscored by the risotto recipes in this book, which range from Italian classics to modern dishes influenced by kitchens from around the world. You'll find risottos that can be served as the centerpiece of a meal and others that make excellent first courses or side dishes. You'll even discover a few contemporary risottos made from grains other than rice. The recipes are organized into chapters by their featured ingredients—vegetables, seafood, and meat and poultry. A final chapter includes shaped risotto dishes.

Another appealing aspect of risotto is how simple it is to make. The following pages cover the basics, including step-by-step instructions for making traditional risotto, a guide to popular herb and cheese additions, and illustrated methods for preparing two of the most common shaped risottos.

These features have a common goal: to make it as easy as possible for you to enjoy flavorful, satisfying risottos at home.

Chuck Williams

RISOTTO BASICS

A specialty of northern Italy, risotto is made with plump grains of particular rice varieties that are slowly simmered in hot liquid until tender but still firm to the bite. During cooking, the surface starch on the grains dissolves to form a thick, creamy sauce. The characteristic mild flavor and creamy consistency of risotto make it an ideal foundation to which other ingredients can be added during cooking. Whatever kind of risotto you make, the same general principles apply.

SELECTING A GRAIN

The rice variety known as Arborio is the primary type used for risotto. Two other varieties are also prized: Carnaroli, which has a somewhat firmer texture than Arborio, and Vialone Nano, a slightly shorter grain that cooks about 5 minutes faster and yields a slightly less creamy sauce. Although they may be harder to find, they are worth seeking out for their distinctive character.

The growing popularity of risotto has led cooks to seek out other grains that can be prepared in a similar way. The most successful substitute is barley, which cooks to a chewy texture while producing its own creamy sauce. Fresh sweet corn can also be cooked in the style of risotto to take advantage of the naturally starchy grain's thickening powers.

SELECTING PANS AND HEATING STOCK

Most risotto recipes begin with two simple but important steps. The first is the choice of a heavy saucepan that holds heat well and is large and wide enough to allow you to stir the risotto easily. The second is the selection of the cooking liquid, which depends upon the particular recipe. Chicken, beef, vegetable, and fish stocks are among the possibilities. Homemade stocks (pages 12–13) are the best choice; good-quality canned or frozen broths are acceptable alternatives, and bottled clam juice may be used in place of fish stock. The liquid is brought to a simmer before adding it to the rice, as hot liquid is absorbed more readily than cold.

COOKING THE RISOTTO

Most risotto recipes call for the brief sautéing of aromatic vegetables such as garlic, onions, or shallots in oil, butter, or a mixture of the two, before the rice is cooked in the stock. This step infuses the relatively bland-tasting grain with a good flavor base. Next, the rice is added and briefly stirred to coat it.

Liquid is added to the rice about a ladleful at a time, with the heat beneath the pan adjusted to maintain a gentle simmer. Although you can take brief breaks to attend to other kitchen chores, nearly constant stirring is important: it keeps the grains in contact with the liquid for even cooking, prevents the rice from sticking to the bottom of the pan, and dislodges surface starch from the rice into the liquid, causing it to thicken.

TESTING FOR DONENESS

Risotto is ready to remove from the heat when the liquid has been absorbed and the grains are tender but still chewy. Cooking times depend on the type of rice used and its age. Start tasting the rice to check for doneness about 20 minutes after you begin adding liquid.

Classic Risotto

Delicious on its own, this recipe can be varied by using Vegetable Stock (page 12) instead of the Chicken Stock or by flavoring it with herbs or another cheese. Classic Risotto is also the foundation for such dishes as Osso Buco on a Bed of Risotto (page 84) and is used to prepare shaped risottos such as pancakes and supplì (pages 93–96).

6 cups (48 fl oz/1.5 l) Chicken Stock (*page 13*) or broth
2 tablespoons unsalted butter
1 yellow onion, chopped
2½ cups (17½ oz/545 g) Arborio rice
⅔ cup (5 fl oz/160 ml) dry white wine
1¾ cups (7 oz/220 g) grated Parmesan cheese
salt and ground pepper to taste

Pour the stock or broth into a saucepan and bring to a simmer. Adjust the heat to keep the liquid hot.

In a large, heavy saucepan over low heat, melt the butter. Add the onion and sauté until translucent, about 8 minutes. Add the rice and stir until white spots appear in the center of the grains, about 1 minute. Add the wine and stir until absorbed, about 2 minutes.

Add one ladleful of the hot stock or broth, adjust the heat to maintain a gentle simmer, and cook, stirring constantly, until the liquid is absorbed, about 2 minutes. Continue adding the stock or broth, one ladleful at a time and stirring constantly, until the rice is just tender but slightly firm in the center and the mixture is creamy, 20–25 minutes longer.

Add the cheese and season with salt and pepper. Stir to mix well.

Spoon into warmed shallow bowls or onto plates, or arrange on a warmed platter, and serve at once.

Makes 6 cups (30 oz/940 g)

Making Risotto

The easy-to-follow recipe at left uses steps that apply to preparing any risotto. Adding the liquid in increments and stirring the rice constantly help ensure a creamy result. You may not need all of the liquid. However, if the liquid has been used up and the rice is still firm, add hot water and cook a little longer, until the rice is done to your taste.

1. Stirring the rice.
After the onion is sautéed, add the rice and stir until white spots appear in the center of the grains. The grains will turn translucent at the edges and be lightly coated with butter.

2. Adding the stock or broth.
Pour in the wine and stir until absorbed. Add a ladleful of the hot stock or broth and stir again until absorbed. Continue adding the hot liquid only after each ladleful is absorbed.

3. Flavoring the risotto.
Sprinkle in the Parmesan cheese. Stir to mix well and allow the cheese to melt and blend with the hot risotto. Taste and adjust the seasoning with salt and pepper.

Seasoning with Herbs

Adding herbs to risotto is one of the easiest ways to give it character. Fresh herbs, which as a rule have a more delicate bouquet than dried herbs, are stirred into risotto as it cooks and are also often sprinkled over the finished dish as a garnish. Dried herbs are acceptable alternatives, although they must be used in smaller amounts because of their more concentrated flavor. To release the flavor of dried herbs, crush them in the palm of the hand before adding them to the risotto.

Keep fresh herbs in the refrigerator, placing the stem ends in water or wrapping the herbs in damp paper towels, and then enclosing in a plastic bag. Dried herbs lose flavor over time, so buy in quantities that you will use within about 6 months, and store in airtight containers, away from heat and light.

Basil. This sweet, spicy herb, best when used fresh but also available dried, is a staple of Italian and French kitchens. It goes especially well with tomatoes and is a key ingredient in pesto sauce (page 36).

Bay Leaves. The dried whole leaves of the bay laurel tree contribute a pungent, spicy flavor to simmered dishes such as homemade stocks used for cooking risotto (pages 12–13) and meats that are cooked with or served on top of risotto, such as osso buco (page 84). The French variety, sometimes available in specialty-food stores, has a milder, sweeter flavor than the more common California bay leaves. Remove and discard the leaves before serving the finished dish.

Chives. This mild, sweet herb with thin, grasslike leaves has a flavor reminiscent of onion, to which it is related. Although chives are available dried, fresh chives have the best flavor.

Cilantro. Resembling flat-leaf parsley, this green, leafy herb has a sharp, aromatic, somewhat astringent flavor that complements risotto featuring seafood. It is also called fresh coriander or Chinese parsley.

Marjoram. Pungent and aromatic, marjoram is used fresh or dried as a seasoning for risottos that include poultry, seafood, vegetables, and eggs.

Oregano. Aromatic and spicy, this herb—also known as wild marjoram—is used fresh or dried in all kinds of savory dishes, particularly those with tomatoes and other vegetables.

Parsley, Flat-Leaf. Perhaps the most popular of fresh herbs, parsley is generally available in two varieties, the common curly-leaf type most often used as a garnish and a flat-leaf type. The latter, also known as Italian parsley, has a much more pronounced flavor that makes it preferred, especially in Mediterranean dishes such as risotto.

Rosemary. This popular herb of the Mediterranean region, used fresh or dried, imparts its strong, aromatic flavor to risotto dishes featuring meat, poultry, seafood, and vegetables.

Sage. Used fresh or dried, sage has a pungent, highly aromatic flavor that makes it especially well suited to meat and poultry risottos.

Tarragon. Distinguished by its long, delicately slender leaves that have a distinctively sweet fragrance, tarragon is used fresh or dried to season dishes featuring seafood, chicken, light meats, eggs, and vegetables.

Thyme. Used fresh or dried, this popular small-leaved herb has a fragrant, clean taste that goes well with poultry, seafood, and vegetables.

FLAVORING WITH CHEESES

Risotto often includes cheese, stirred into the rice shortly before it is served. The cheese enriches and adds body to the rice, as well as flavoring it. Many cheeses are used in risotto and as a filling for the shaped risotto specialty known as supplì; the varieties called for in this book are described below. Bear in mind that most cheeses are fairly salty, requiring you to exercise restraint when seasoning with salt.

Before adding semifirm cheeses such as fontina to risotto, they are shredded, using the medium or large holes of a handheld grater or a food processor fitted with the shredding attachment, or are finely diced. Hard cheeses like Parmesan are grated on the fine rasps of the grater. Shavings of Parmesan, used for garnish, can be cut with a vegetable peeler or cheese shaver.

Feta. This Mediterranean white cheese, traditionally made from sheep's or goat's milk, and now also made from cow's milk, is notable for its salty, sharp flavor and creamy to dry consistency. Crumble feta before adding to risotto.

Fontina. This semifirm, creamy, delicate cow's milk cheese has a pleasantly nutty flavor with hints of honey. Look for genuine fontina from the Aosta Valley of northwestern Italy, which is superior to fontina-style cheeses from other countries. Fontina may be shredded or finely diced for adding to risotto. It is also cut into small pieces for supplì filling.

Goat Cheese. Cheeses made from goat's milk, often known by the French term *chèvre,* are available fresh, with a mildly tangy flavor and creamy white consistency, or aged to a sharper taste and ivory color. Goat cheeses are often sold shaped into small rounds or logs, and both fresh and aged goat cheeses may be coated with herbs, ground pepper, or wood ash, which mildly flavors the cheese. Almost all goat cheeses may be crumbled by hand for blending easily with risotto.

Gorgonzola. This creamy, semisoft, blue-veined cheese made from cow's milk comes from the Lombardy region of Italy. The mildest, creamiest versions are called gorgonzola dolcelatte, meaning "sweet milk." Other mild blue cheeses may be substituted. The cheese is usually crumbled before being added to risotto.

Gouda. A buttery, semisoft Dutch cheese, Gouda is golden yellow and has a flavor that ranges from mild when aged for just 2 months to strong and spicy when aged for 4 months or longer. Edam cheese may be substituted. Shred Gouda before adding to risotto.

Mozzarella. A rindless white, mild-tasting Italian cheese, mozzarella is traditionally made from water buffalo's milk and sold fresh, floating in water, and sometimes labeled "mozzarella di bufala." Cow's milk mozzarella is more common, although it has a less delicate flavor and texture and a lower water content. Mozzarella is also sometimes smoked, yielding a firmer-textured, aromatic but still mild-tasting cheese. Shred all kinds of mozzarella for use in risotto. It is also diced or cubed as a filling for supplì.

Parmesan. A firm cheese made from a mixture of skimmed and whole cow's milk, Parmesan has a sharp, salty, nutlike flavor that results from up to 2 years of aging. In its prime, a good piece of Parmesan cheese is dry but not grainy and flakes easily. For the best flavor, buy imported Italian Parmesan in block form; the finest variety is designated Parmigiano-Reggiano®. Finely grate the cheese as needed.

Pecorino. Made from sheep's milk, this venerable Italian cheese is sold in both fresh and aged forms. Two of the most popular aged forms are pecorino romano and pecorino sardo; the latter has a tangier flavor. Pecorino may be used much like Parmesan. Buy it in block form and grate as needed.

9

Making Risotto Pancakes

These simple pancakes from the recipe on page 93 can be prepared with leftover risotto or with the Classic Risotto (page 7). Using a nonstick frying pan helps prevent sticking. Accompany with additional Parmesan cheese or with Tomato Sauce (page 12).

1. Adding the risotto to the pan.
Place a large frying pan over medium heat and melt 1 tablespoon butter. For each pancake, drop about ⅓ cup (1¾ oz/52 g) of the risotto into the pan.

2. Shaping the pancakes.
Using a spatula, carefully press each mound of risotto into a flat round.

3. Turning the pancakes.
Fry the pancakes until light brown on the bottom, about 3 minutes. Use the spatula to turn the pancakes. Add more butter as needed to prevent sticking.

4. Sprinkling on the cheese.
After each pancake is turned, sprinkle the top with 1 tablespoon Parmesan cheese.

5. Melting the cheese.
Cover the pan and cook the pancakes until the cheese melts, about 1 minute. Uncover and continue frying until the pancakes are light brown on the bottom, about 2 minutes longer.

MAKING SUPPLÌ

Risotto, combined with eggs and sometimes bread crumbs to give it body, can be shaped around a variety of fillings and then fried to made supplì, a traditional Italian dish. Follow these simple steps for preparing Supplì with Fontina and Porcini (page 94) and the other supplì in this book.

4. Frying the supplì.
Heat 2 inches (5 cm) of oil in a saucepan until a bit of bread turns golden when dropped into the oil. Add the formed supplì and fry, turning as needed, until uniformly golden brown, about 3 minutes.

1. Adding the risotto to the bread crumbs.
Place the bread crumbs in a pie plate. Scoop up 1 tablespoon of the risotto and drop it into the crumbs. Using two fingers, make a slight indentation in the risotto.

5. Draining the supplì.
As the supplì are done, use a slotted spoon to transfer them to a baking sheet lined with paper towels to drain. Slip into a 250°F (120°C) oven to keep warm while frying the remaining supplì.

2. Adding the filling.
Place the filling—here, a small piece of fontina cheese and 1 teaspoon chopped porcini mushrooms—in the indentation. Top with 1 tablespoon of the risotto.

3. Shaping and coating the supplì.
Using your hands, carefully form the risotto into a cylinder, enclosing the filling. Roll the cylinder in the bread crumbs to coat evenly, and place on a waxed paper–lined baking sheet.

11

Tomato Sauce

This sauce has a spicy, fresh flavor well suited for use in Supplì with Smoked Ham and Mozzarella (page 96) and for serving with this and other supplì and shaped risotto dishes in this book. If fresh sweet tomatoes are unavailable, good-quality canned tomatoes will work well.

2 tablespoons olive oil
1 yellow onion, chopped
8 tomatoes, peeled, seeded, and chopped, or 1 can (28 oz/875 g) plum (Roma) tomatoes, drained and chopped
1 teaspoon chopped fresh oregano or ½ teaspoon dried oregano
large pinch of red pepper flakes
2 tablespoons balsamic vinegar
1 tablespoon tomato paste
¼ cup (2 fl oz/60 ml) dry red wine
½ teaspoon sugar
salt and ground pepper to taste

*I*n a large frying pan over medium heat, warm the olive oil. Add the onion and sauté until soft, about 10 minutes.

Add the tomatoes, oregano, red pepper flakes, vinegar, tomato paste, wine, and sugar. Season with salt and pepper. Bring to a simmer and cook gently, uncovered, until the sauce thickens, about 20 minutes. Stir two or three times during cooking to prevent scorching. Remove from the heat and let cool.

If a smooth sauce is desired, transfer to a blender or food processor and purée. Taste and adjust the seasonings with salt and pepper. Use the sauce hot or at room temperature. Store in a tightly covered container in the refrigerator for up to 3 days or in the freezer for up to 2 months.

Makes about 2 cups (16 fl oz/500 ml)

Vegetable Stock

Use this simple stock for a vegetarian risotto or, if desired, as a substitute for Chicken Stock.

3 large yellow onions, cut into 1-inch (2.5-cm) pieces
4 large carrots, peeled and cut into 1-inch (2.5-cm) pieces
4 celery stalks with leaves, cut into 1-inch (2.5-cm) pieces
4 fresh parsley sprigs
1 bay leaf
3 qt (3 l) water

*I*n a large saucepan, combine the onions, carrots, celery, parsley, and bay leaf. Pour in the water and bring to a boil over medium heat. Reduce the heat to low and simmer, uncovered, for 1 hour. Skim off any scum or froth that rises to the surface.

Strain the stock through a colander or sieve placed over a large bowl. Discard the solids and let the stock cool to room temperature. Store in a tightly covered container in the refrigerator for up to 3 days or in the freezer for up to 3 months.

Makes about 7 cups (56 fl oz/1.75 l)

Fish Stock

This flavorful stock is ideal for seafood risottos. Bottled clam juice may be substituted.

3 lb (1.5 kg) fish bones, heads, and skin from nonoily fish such as cod, sole, snapper, halibut, sea bass, or monkfish
2 yellow onions, cut into 1-inch (2.5-cm) pieces
3 celery stalks with leaves, cut into 1-inch (2.5-cm) pieces
2 cups (16 fl oz/500 ml) dry white wine
7 cups (56 fl oz/1.75 l) water

Remove any scales from the fish skin. Remove the gills from the fish heads. Rinse the bones, heads, and skin.

In a large saucepan, combine the fish parts, onions, and celery. Pour in the wine and water. Bring to a boil over medium heat, skimming the surface occasionally to remove any scum or froth. Reduce the heat to low and simmer, uncovered, for 30 minutes. Continue to skim off the froth that rises to the surface.

Strain the stock through a colander or sieve lined with a double thickness of cheesecloth (muslin) and placed over a large bowl. Discard the solids. Store the stock in a tightly covered container in the refrigerator for up to 3 days or in the freezer for up to 1 month.

Makes about 6 cups (48 fl oz/1.5 l)

Chicken Stock

Prepare this stock in advance so you have it on hand for making many of the risotto dishes in this book. In place of homemade stock, substitute canned low-sodium broth, which offers greater leeway for seasoning than salted versions.

3 lb (1.5 kg) chicken backs and necks
2 large yellow onions, cut into 1-inch (2.5-cm) pieces
2 large carrots, peeled and cut into 1-inch (2.5-cm) pieces
2 bay leaves
4 fresh parsley sprigs
3 qt (3 l) water

In a large saucepan, combine the chicken, onions, carrots, bay leaves, and parsley. Pour in the water and bring to a boil over medium heat, skimming the surface occasionally to remove any scum or froth.

Reduce the heat to low, cover partially, and simmer for 3 hours. Continue to skim off any froth that rises to the surface.

Strain the stock through a colander or sieve lined with a double thickness of cheesecloth (muslin) and placed over a large bowl. Discard the solids and refrigerate the stock until the fat solidifies on the surface. Lift off the fat and discard. Store the stock in a tightly covered container in the refrigerator for up to 3 days or in the freezer for up to 3 months.

Makes about 8 cups (64 fl oz/2 l)

Asparagus Risotto

5½ cups (44 fl oz/1.35 l) Chicken Stock
 (*page 13*), Vegetable Stock (*page 12*),
 or broth
1¼ lb (625 g) asparagus, cut into
 1½-inch (4-cm) lengths
¾ cup (6 fl oz/180 ml) dry white wine
2 tablespoons olive oil
1 yellow onion, chopped
2 cups (14 oz/440 g) Arborio rice
1 cup (4 oz/125 g) grated Parmesan
 cheese
1 tablespoon finely chopped fresh
 tarragon, plus fresh sprigs for garnish
salt and ground pepper to taste

Prepare this dish when springtime asparagus is at its best. If you wish, substitute another herb for the tarragon, such as chervil or dill. A little grated lemon zest also nicely complements the vegetable.

*I*n a saucepan over high heat, bring the stock or broth to a boil. Add the asparagus and boil until just tender-crisp, about 2 minutes. Using a slotted spoon, transfer to a bowl and set aside.

Add the wine to the stock or broth and bring to a simmer. Adjust the heat to keep the liquid hot.

In a large, heavy saucepan over medium-low heat, warm the olive oil. Add the onion and sauté until translucent, about 8 minutes. Add the rice and stir until white spots appear in the center of the grains, about 1 minute. Add a ladleful of the liquid, adjust the heat to maintain a simmer, and cook, stirring constantly, until the liquid is absorbed, about 2 minutes. Continue adding the liquid, a ladleful at a time and stirring constantly, until the rice is just tender but slightly firm in the center and the mixture is creamy, 20–25 minutes longer.

Add the asparagus, Parmesan cheese, and chopped tarragon and season with salt and pepper. Stir to mix well.

To serve, spoon onto warmed individual plates and garnish with tarragon sprigs.

Serves 4

Ratatouille Risotto

8 cups (64 fl oz/2 l) Vegetable Stock
  (page 12) or broth
¼ cup (2 fl oz/60 ml) extra-virgin
  olive oil
2 cloves garlic, minced
1 yellow onion, chopped
2 Asian (slender) eggplants (aubergines),
  trimmed, halved lengthwise, and
  then cut crosswise into slices ½ inch
  (12 mm) thick
2 zucchini (courgettes), trimmed, halved
  lengthwise, and then cut crosswise into
  slices ½ inch (12 mm) thick
2½ cups (17½ oz/545 g) Arborio rice
4 plum (Roma) tomatoes, seeded and
  coarsely chopped
2 tablespoons tomato paste
1½ tablespoons dried oregano
1 tablespoon sugar
6 tablespoons (½ oz/15 g) finely
  shredded fresh basil leaves
½ cup (2 oz/60 g) grated Parmesan
  cheese
salt and ground pepper to taste
¼ lb (125 g) fresh goat cheese, crumbled

The flavors of the popular southern French vegetable dish permeate this vegetarian risotto, which may be enjoyed on its own as a main course or served alongside grilled meat, particularly lamb.

Pour the stock or broth into a saucepan and bring to a simmer. Adjust the heat to keep the liquid hot.

In a large, heavy saucepan over medium heat, warm the olive oil. Add the garlic and onion and sauté until they begin to turn translucent, about 3 minutes. Raise the heat to high, add the eggplant and zucchini, and sauté just until they begin to take on some color, about 5 minutes longer. Reduce the heat to medium, add the rice, and stir until white spots appear at the center of the grains, about 1 minute. Add a ladleful of the stock or broth along with the tomatoes, tomato paste, oregano, sugar, and 3 tablespoons of the basil. Stir well, then adjust the heat to maintain a simmer and cook, stirring constantly, until the liquid is absorbed, about 2 minutes. Continue adding the liquid, a ladleful at a time and stirring the rice constantly, until the rice is just tender but slightly firm in the center and the mixture is creamy, 20–25 minutes longer.

Add the Parmesan cheese and season with salt and pepper. Stir to mix well.

To serve, spoon onto a warmed platter. Sprinkle with the goat cheese. Garnish with the remaining 3 tablespoons basil.

Serves 6

Risotto with Tomatoes and Basil

3 cups (24 fl oz/750 ml) Chicken Stock
   (page 13) or broth
3 cups (24 fl oz/750 ml) water
1½ cups (9 oz/280 g) peeled, seeded, and
   chopped fresh tomatoes
3 tablespoons extra-virgin olive oil
1 yellow onion, finely chopped
1½ cups (10½ oz/330 g) Arborio rice
3 oz (90 g) dry-packed sun-dried
   tomatoes, cut into bite-sized pieces
1½ tablespoons balsamic vinegar
2 cloves garlic, finely chopped
3 tablespoons finely chopped fresh
   flat-leaf (Italian) parsley
salt and ground pepper to taste
20 fresh basil leaves, cut into thin strips

Tomatoes play two distinct roles in this colorful risotto. Chopped fresh tomatoes are added to the stock, giving the dish an overall rosy hue, while their sun-dried counterparts, added near the end, deliver an intense tomato flavor.

*P*our the stock or broth and the water into a saucepan and add the chopped fresh tomatoes. Bring to a simmer and adjust the heat to keep the liquid hot.

In a heavy saucepan over medium heat, warm the olive oil. Add the onion and sauté until soft, about 10 minutes. Add the rice and stir until white spots appear in the center of the grains, about 1 minute. Add a ladleful of the liquid, adjust the heat to maintain a simmer, and cook, stirring constantly, until the liquid is absorbed, about 2 minutes. Continue adding the liquid, a ladleful at a time and stirring constantly, until the rice starts to soften, about 10 minutes.

Stir in the sun-dried tomatoes and continue adding the liquid, a ladleful at a time and stirring constantly, until the rice is just tender but still slightly firm in the center, the mixture is creamy, and only one ladleful of liquid remains, 10–15 minutes longer.

Stir in the remaining ladleful of liquid and the vinegar, garlic, and parsley. Season with salt and pepper.

Spoon onto warmed individual plates, garnish with the basil, and serve.

Serves 6

Porcini, Caramelized Onion, and Sage Risotto

¾ oz (20 g) dried porcini mushrooms
1 cup (8 fl oz/250 ml) hot water
5½ cups (44 fl oz/1.35 l) Chicken Stock
   (*page 13*), Vegetable Stock (*page 12*),
   or broth
2 tablespoons unsalted butter
2 tablespoons olive oil
2 yellow onions, quartered lengthwise
   and sliced crosswise
2 cups (14 oz/440 g) Arborio rice
¾ cup (6 fl oz/180 ml) dry white wine
1 tablespoon finely chopped fresh sage or
   1 teaspoon dried sage, plus whole fresh
   leaves for garnish (optional)
1½ cups (6 oz/185 g) grated Parmesan
   cheese
salt and ground pepper to taste

The earthiness of Italy's beloved dried porcini mushrooms, the sweetness of onions, and the sharp perfume of sage add up to a classic risotto. Other dried mushrooms may be substituted for the porcini.

◈

*I*n a small bowl, combine the mushrooms and the hot water. Let stand for 30 minutes to soften. Using a slotted spoon, remove the mushrooms from the soaking liquid. Chop the mushrooms. Line a sieve with cheesecloth (muslin) and pour the liquid through it into a clean bowl. Set the chopped mushrooms and strained liquid aside separately.

Pour the stock or broth into a saucepan and bring to a simmer. Adjust the heat to keep the liquid hot.

In a large, heavy saucepan over medium-high heat, melt the butter with the olive oil. Add the onions and sauté until browned, about 10 minutes. Add the rice and mushrooms and stir until white spots appear in the center of the grains, about 1 minute. Add the wine and stir until absorbed, about 2 minutes. Add the chopped or dried sage, the mushroom soaking liquid, and a ladleful of the stock or broth. Reduce the heat to maintain a simmer and cook, stirring constantly, until the liquid is absorbed. Continue adding the liquid, a ladleful at a time and stirring constantly, until the rice is just tender but slightly firm in the center and the mixture is creamy, 20–25 minutes longer.

Add the Parmesan cheese and season with salt and pepper. Stir to mix well.

To serve, spoon onto a warmed platter and garnish with sage leaves, if using.

Serves 4

Risotto with Mozzarella and Sun-Dried Tomatoes

5½ cups (44 fl oz/1.35 l) Chicken Stock (page 13), Vegetable Stock (page 12), or broth

⅓ cup (3 oz/90 g) oil-packed sun-dried tomatoes

1 yellow onion, chopped

2 cups (14 oz/440 g) Arborio rice

1 cup (4 oz/125 g) finely shredded mozzarella cheese (see note)

1 cup (4 oz/125 g) grated Parmesan cheese

¼ cup (⅓ oz/10 g) finely chopped fresh basil, plus whole leaves for garnish

salt and ground pepper to taste

Use fresh mozzarella cheese, packed in water, for the best result. It will melt into threads, giving the risotto an intriguing texture.

*P*our the stock or broth into a saucepan and bring to a simmer. Adjust the heat to keep the liquid hot.

Drain the sun-dried tomatoes and reserve the oil. Add more oil from the jar to equal 4 tablespoons (2 fl oz/60 ml). Chop the sun-dried tomatoes and set aside.

In a large, heavy saucepan over medium-low heat, warm 2 tablespoons of the oil. Add the onion and sauté until translucent, about 8 minutes. Add the rice and stir until white spots appear in the center of the grains, about 1 minute. Add a ladleful of the stock or broth, adjust the heat to maintain a simmer, and cook, stirring constantly, until the liquid is absorbed, about 2 minutes. Continue adding the liquid, a ladleful at a time and stirring constantly, until the rice is just tender but slightly firm in the center and the mixture is creamy, 20–25 minutes longer.

Add the mozzarella cheese, Parmesan cheese, sun-dried tomatoes, chopped basil, and remaining 2 tablespoons oil and season with salt and pepper. Stir to mix well.

To serve, spoon onto warmed individual plates and garnish with the basil leaves.

Serves 6

Risotto with Greens, Gorgonzola, and Walnuts

½ cup (2 oz/60 g) walnuts

5 cups (40 fl oz/1.25 l) Chicken Stock
(page 13), Vegetable Stock (page 12),
or broth

3 tablespoons olive oil

½ large yellow onion, chopped

1½ cups (10½ oz/330 g) Arborio rice

½ cup (4 fl oz/125 ml) dry white wine

3 cups (6 oz/185 g) thinly sliced greens
such as escarole (Batavian endive),
Swiss chard, kale, or beet

¾ cup (4 oz/125 g) crumbled Gorgonzola
cheese

salt and ground pepper to taste

The combination of robust greens, tangy cheese, and toasted nuts makes this an ideal prelude to simple roast poultry. Substitute Roquefort, Danish blue, or another blue-veined cheese for the Gorgonzola.

Preheat an oven to 325°F (165°C). Spread the walnuts on a baking sheet and toast in the oven until lightly colored and fragrant, 5–7 minutes. Let cool, chop coarsely, and set aside.

Pour the stock or broth into a saucepan and bring to a simmer. Adjust the heat to keep the liquid hot.

In a heavy saucepan over medium-low heat, warm the olive oil. Add the onion and sauté until translucent, about 8 minutes. Add the rice and stir until white spots appear in the center of the grains, about 1 minute. Add the wine and stir until absorbed, about 2 minutes. Add a ladleful of the stock or broth, adjust the heat to maintain a simmer, and cook, stirring constantly, until the liquid is absorbed. Continue adding the liquid, a ladleful at a time and stirring constantly, until the rice starts to soften, about 10 minutes.

Add the greens and continue adding the liquid, a ladleful at a time and stirring constantly, until the rice is just tender but slightly firm in the center and the mixture is creamy, 10–15 minutes longer.

Add the Gorgonzola cheese and walnuts and season with salt and pepper. Stir to mix well.

To serve, spoon into warmed individual bowls.

Serves 4

Red and Yellow Pepper Risotto with Fontina

5 cups (40 fl oz/1.25 l) Chicken Stock
(page 13), Vegetable Stock (page 12),
or broth
2 tablespoons olive oil
1 large yellow onion, chopped
1 red bell pepper (capsicum), seeded and
cut into ½-inch (12-mm) squares
1 yellow bell pepper (capsicum), seeded
and cut into ½-inch (12-mm) squares
1 clove garlic, minced
1½ cups (10½ oz/330 g) Arborio rice
¾ cup (3 oz/90 g) shredded fontina
cheese
1 tablespoon chopped fresh thyme
salt and ground pepper to taste

Contrasting colors of bell peppers give this risotto flecks of bright color and sweet flavor. For an equally delicious variation, use shredded Gouda cheese in place of the fontina.

Pour the stock or broth into a saucepan and bring to a simmer. Adjust the heat to keep the liquid hot.

In a heavy saucepan over medium-low heat, warm the olive oil. Add the onion and sauté until it begins to soften, about 5 minutes. Add the red and yellow bell peppers and the garlic and sauté until the peppers begin to soften, about 5 minutes. Add the rice and stir until white spots appear in the center of the grains, about 1 minute. Add a ladleful of the stock or broth, adjust the heat to maintain a simmer, and cook, stirring constantly, until the liquid is absorbed, about 2 minutes. Continue adding the liquid, a ladleful at a time and stirring constantly, until the rice is just tender but slightly firm in the center and the mixture is creamy, 20–25 minutes longer.

Add the fontina cheese and thyme and stir until the cheese melts. Season with salt and pepper.

To serve, spoon onto warmed individual plates.

Serves 4

Spinach Risotto

½ lb (250 g) spinach

4½ cups (36 fl oz/1.1 l) Chicken Stock (*page 13*) or broth

½ cup (4 fl oz/125 ml) dry white wine

6 tablespoons (3 oz/90 g) unsalted butter

2 cups (14 oz/440 g) Arborio rice

salt and ground pepper to taste

½ cup (2 oz/60 g) grated Parmesan cheese

Here, spinach is cooked separately and then stirred into the creamy risotto at the last minute along with a little butter.

Rinse the spinach thoroughly, remove the stems, and place in a saucepan with water still clinging to the leaves. Cover and place over medium heat until just wilted, about 1 minute. Drain well, pressing any liquid from the leaves. Chop coarsely and set aside.

Pour the stock or broth and the wine into a saucepan and bring to a simmer. Adjust the heat to keep the liquid hot.

In a large, heavy saucepan over medium-low heat, melt 4 tablespoons of the butter. Add the rice and stir until white spots appear in the center of the grains, about 1 minute. Add a ladleful of the stock or broth, adjust the heat to maintain a simmer, and cook, stirring constantly, until the liquid is absorbed, about 2 minutes. Continue adding the liquid, a ladleful at a time and stirring constantly, until the rice is just tender but slightly firm in the center and the mixture is creamy, 20–25 minutes.

Add the remaining 2 tablespoons butter and the chopped spinach and season with salt and pepper. Stir to mix well.

Spoon the risotto into warmed individual bowls, top with the cheese, and serve.

Serves 6

Butternut Squash, Sage, and Hazelnut Risotto

¼ cup (1¼ oz/37 g) hazelnuts (filberts)

5½ cups (44 fl oz/1.35 l) Chicken Stock (*page 13*), Vegetable Stock (*page 12*), or broth

2 tablespoons unsalted butter

1 large yellow onion, chopped

1 butternut squash or other orange-fleshed squash (about 1½ lb/750 g), halved, seeded, peeled, and cubed

5 teaspoons chopped fresh sage or 1 teaspoon dried sage

1½ cups (10½ oz/330 g) Arborio rice

½ cup (4 fl oz/125 ml) dry white wine

⅓ cup (1½ oz/45 g) grated Parmesan cheese

1½ teaspoons ground pepper

salt to taste

With its autumnal colors and flavors, this risotto is ideal served alongside a main course of grilled pork chops.

Preheat an oven to 325°F (165°C). Spread the hazelnuts on a baking sheet and toast in the oven until fragrant and the skins have loosened, 5–7 minutes. Remove from the oven and, while still warm, place the nuts in a kitchen towel. Rub vigorously to remove the skins. Chop coarsely and set aside.

Pour the stock or broth into a saucepan and bring to a simmer. Adjust the heat to keep the liquid hot.

In a heavy saucepan over low heat, melt the butter. Add the onion and sauté until soft, about 10 minutes. Add the squash and 4 teaspoons of the fresh sage or all of the dried sage and sauté until the squash is hot, about 2 minutes. Cover and cook until the squash is almost tender, about 6 minutes.

Uncover, add the rice, and stir until white spots appear in the center of the grains, about 1 minute. Add the wine and stir until absorbed, about 2 minutes. Add a ladleful of the stock or broth, adjust the heat to maintain a simmer, and cook, stirring constantly, until the liquid is absorbed. Continue adding the liquid, a ladleful at a time and stirring constantly, until the rice is just tender but slightly firm in the center and the mixture is creamy, 20–25 minutes longer.

Add the Parmesan cheese, all but 1 tablespoon of the chopped nuts, and the pepper, and season with salt. Stir to mix well.

To serve, spoon into warmed individual bowls and garnish with the remaining 1 teaspoon fresh sage, if using, and the remaining 1 tablespoon nuts.

Serves 6

Pea, Tarragon, and Goat Cheese Risotto

5½ cups (44 fl oz/1.35 l) Chicken Stock
   (page 13), Vegetable Stock (page 12),
   or broth
3 tablespoons olive oil
½ large yellow onion, chopped
1½ cups (10½ oz/330 g) Arborio rice
½ cup (4 fl oz/125 ml) dry white wine
1½ cups (7½ oz/235 g) shelled fresh or
   thawed frozen English peas
2 teaspoons finely chopped fresh
   tarragon, plus fresh sprigs for garnish
½ cup (2½ oz/75 g) crumbled fresh
   goat cheese
salt and ground pepper to taste

A contemporary version of the Venetian specialty risi e bisi—*a cross between risotto and soup—this recipe replaces the traditional Parmesan with goat cheese and cooks the dish to a slightly thicker consistency.*

Pour the stock or broth into a saucepan and bring to a simmer. Adjust the heat to low to keep the liquid hot.

In a heavy saucepan over medium-low heat, warm the olive oil. Add the onion and sauté until translucent, about 8 minutes. Add the rice and stir until white spots appear in the center of the grains, about 1 minute. Add the wine and stir until absorbed, about 2 minutes. Add a ladleful of the stock or broth, adjust the heat to maintain a simmer, and cook, stirring constantly, until the liquid is absorbed. Continue adding the liquid, a ladleful at a time and stirring constantly, until the rice starts to soften, 10–15 minutes.

Add the peas and chopped tarragon and continue adding the liquid, a ladleful at a time and stirring constantly, until the rice is just tender but slightly firm in the center and the mixture is creamy, 10–15 minutes longer.

Add the goat cheese and stir until the cheese melts. Season with salt and pepper.

To serve, spoon onto warmed individual plates and garnish with the tarragon sprigs.

Serves 4

Broccoli Risotto with Parmesan

5½ cups (44 fl oz/1.35 l) Chicken Stock
   (*page 13*), Vegetable Stock (*page 12*),
   or broth
2 tablespoons olive oil
1 yellow onion, chopped
1½ cups (10½ oz/330 g) Arborio rice
4 cups (12 oz/375 g) broccoli florets
1 cup (4 oz/125 g) grated Parmesan
   cheese, plus additional cheese for
   serving
salt and ground pepper to taste

You'll get the right amount of florets for this dish if you purchase about 1 pound (500 g) broccoli (reserve the stalks for another recipe). Try substituting Gorgonzola or pecorino romano cheese for the Parmesan.

Pour the stock or broth into a saucepan and bring to a simmer. Adjust the heat to keep the liquid hot.

In a heavy saucepan over medium-low heat, warm the olive oil. Add the onion and sauté until translucent, about 8 minutes. Add the rice and stir until white spots appear in the center of the grains, about 1 minute. Add a ladleful of the stock or broth, adjust the heat to maintain a simmer, and cook, stirring constantly, until the liquid is absorbed, about 2 minutes. Continue adding the liquid, a ladleful at a time and stirring constantly, until the rice starts to soften, 10–15 minutes.

Add the broccoli and continue adding the liquid, a ladleful at a time and stirring constantly, until the rice is just tender but slightly firm in the center and the mixture is creamy, 10–15 minutes longer.

Add the 1 cup (4 oz/125 g) Parmesan cheese and season with salt and pepper. Stir to mix well.

To serve, spoon onto a warmed serving dish. Pass the additional Parmesan cheese at the table.

Serves 4

Lima Bean Risotto with Pesto

FOR THE PESTO:

2 tablespoons pine nuts

½ cup (½ oz/15 g) fresh basil leaves

¼ cup (2 fl oz/60 ml) olive oil

⅓ cup (1½ oz/45 g) grated Parmesan
   cheese

1 clove garlic

5½ cups (44 fl oz/1.35 l) Chicken Stock
   (*page 13*), Vegetable Stock (*page 12*),
   or broth

2 tablespoons olive oil

1 yellow onion, chopped

2½ cups (17½ oz/545 g) Arborio rice

⅔ cup (5 fl oz/160 ml) dry white wine

1 package (10 oz/315 g) frozen baby lima
   beans, thawed

½ cup (2 oz/60 g) grated pecorino
   romano cheese

salt and ground pepper to taste

*There's nothing fancy here, just simple ingredients that combine to
make a risotto with an intriguing color and flavor. Using purchased
pesto will make the recipe even easier.*

To make the pesto, put the pine nuts in a small, dry frying pan
over medium-low heat and toast, stirring constantly, until light
golden brown, 3–5 minutes. Transfer to a plate to cool. In a food
processor or blender, combine the basil, olive oil, Parmesan cheese,
garlic, and toasted nuts. Process until finely ground. Set aside.

Pour the stock or broth into a saucepan and bring to a simmer.
Adjust the heat to keep the liquid hot.

In a large, heavy saucepan over medium-low heat, warm
the olive oil. Add the onion and sauté until translucent, about
8 minutes. Add the rice and stir until white spots appear in the
center of the grains, about 1 minute. Add the wine and stir until
absorbed, about 2 minutes. Add a ladleful of the stock or broth,
adjust the heat to maintain a simmer, and cook, stirring
constantly, until the liquid is absorbed. Continue adding the
liquid, a ladleful at a time and stirring constantly, for 5 minutes.

Add the lima beans and continue adding the liquid, a ladleful
at a time and stirring constantly, until the rice is just tender
but slightly firm in the center and the mixture is creamy,
15–20 minutes longer.

Add the pesto and pecorino romano cheese and season with
salt and pepper. Stir to mix well.

To serve, spoon onto warmed individual plates.

Serves 4

Arugula Risotto with Parmesan

5½ cups (44 fl oz/1.35 l) Chicken Stock (*page 13*), Vegetable Stock (*page 12*), or broth
2 tablespoons olive oil
½ large yellow onion, chopped
2 cups (14 oz/440 g) Arborio rice
1½ cups (6 oz/185 g) grated Parmesan cheese
1⅓ cups (2 oz/60 g) finely chopped arugula (rocket) or watercress, plus sprigs for garnish
salt and ground pepper to taste

Used as both an herb and a salad green, arugula has a peppery taste that adds distinction to this simple dish. If you can't find arugula, watercress also works well.

Pour the stock or broth into a saucepan and bring to a simmer. Adjust the heat to keep the liquid hot.

In a large, heavy saucepan over medium-low heat, warm the olive oil. Add the onion and sauté until translucent, about 8 minutes. Add the rice and stir until white spots appear in the center of the grains, about 1 minute. Add a ladleful of the stock or broth, adjust the heat to maintain a simmer, and cook, stirring constantly, until the liquid is absorbed, about 2 minutes. Continue adding the liquid, a ladleful at a time and stirring constantly, until the rice is just tender but slightly firm in the center and the mixture is creamy, 20–25 minutes longer.

Add the Parmesan cheese and chopped arugula or watercress and season with salt and pepper. Stir to mix well.

To serve, spoon into a warmed serving bowl and garnish with the arugula or watercress sprigs.

Serves 4

Mushroom-Barley Risotto with Seared Portobello Caps

6½ cups (52 fl oz/1.6 l) Vegetable Stock (*page 12*) or broth

4½ tablespoons (2¼ oz/67 g) unsalted butter

4½ tablespoons (2½ fl oz/75 ml) olive oil

4 shallots, minced

1 lb (500 g) fresh cremini mushrooms, brushed clean and thinly sliced

2¼ cups (15 oz/470 g) pearl barley

¾ cup (3 oz/90 g) grated Parmesan cheese

salt and ground pepper to taste

6 large portobello mushrooms, brushed clean and stems trimmed even with bottom of caps

3 tablespoons finely shredded fresh basil leaves

The idea for this vegetarian risotto comes from classic deli-style mushroom-barley soup. To finish the dish, whole portobello mushroom caps are quickly cooked and placed atop each serving.

Pour the stock or broth into a saucepan and bring to a boil. Remove from the heat.

In large, a heavy saucepan over medium-low heat, melt 1½ tablespoons of the butter with 1½ tablespoons of the olive oil. Add the shallots and sauté until translucent, about 2 minutes. Raise the heat to high, add the cremini mushrooms, and sauté until they just begin to turn golden, about 3 minutes. Add the barley and stir for about 30 seconds longer.

Stir in 4½ cups (36 fl oz/1.1 l) of the stock or broth and adjust the heat to maintain a brisk simmer. Cook the barley, stirring frequently, for about 10 minutes. Stir in the remaining 2 cups (16 fl oz/500 ml) stock or broth and continue to simmer, stirring frequently, just until the barley is tender and creamy, about 15 minutes longer. Add the Parmesan cheese and season with salt and pepper. Stir to mix well. Cover and set aside.

In 1 or 2 frying pans large enough to hold the portobello mushrooms in a single layer, melt the remaining 3 tablespoons butter with the remaining 3 tablespoons oil over high heat. As soon as the butter foams, generously sprinkle the pan(s) with salt and pepper and add the mushrooms, hollow sides up. Season the hollows with salt and pepper. Cook, turning once, until seared and heated through, 2–3 minutes on each side.

To serve, spoon the barley risotto into warmed individual bowls. Arrange the portobello caps on top and garnish with the basil.

Serves 6

Risotto with Artichokes and Parmesan

juice of 1 lemon, plus 1 lemon, cut into
   wedges (optional)
4 large artichokes
2 tablespoons extra-virgin olive oil
1 very small yellow onion, minced
2 cloves garlic, minced
½ cup (¾ oz/20 g) chopped fresh parsley
2½ cups (20 fl oz/625 ml) water
pinch of salt, plus salt to taste
3 cups (24 fl oz/750 ml) Chicken Stock
   (*page 13*) or broth
1½ cups (10½ oz/330 g) Arborio rice
½ cup (2 oz/60 g) grated Parmesan
   cheese
ground pepper to taste

*H*ave ready a large bowl of water to which you have added half of the lemon juice. Remove the tough outer leaves of the artichokes. Trim off the stems and the prickly leaf points. Cut in half lengthwise, then scoop out the prickly chokes and discard. Cut the artichokes lengthwise into thin slices. As each is cut, place in the bowl of lemon water.

In a deep frying pan over medium heat, warm the olive oil. Add the onion and sauté until soft, about 10 minutes. Add the garlic and half of the parsley and sauté until the garlic is translucent, about 2 minutes. Drain the artichokes and add to the pan along with ½ cup (4 fl oz/125 ml) of the water and a large pinch of salt. Cover and cook over medium heat until the liquid evaporates, about 25 minutes.

Meanwhile, pour the stock or broth and the remaining 2 cups (16 fl oz/500 ml) water into a saucepan and bring to a simmer. Adjust the heat to keep the liquid hot.

Uncover the artichokes, add the rice, and stir until white spots appear in the center of the grains, about 1 minute. Add a ladleful of the liquid, reduce the heat to maintain a simmer, and cook, stirring constantly, until the liquid is absorbed, about 2 minutes. Continue adding the liquid, a ladleful at a time and stirring constantly, until the rice is just tender but slightly firm in the center and the mixture is creamy, 20–25 minutes longer.

Add the Parmesan cheese and the remaining parsley and lemon juice, and season with salt and pepper. Stir to mix well.

Spoon into warmed individual bowls and serve. Pass the lemon wedges at the table, if desired.

Serves 6

Beet and Goat Cheese Risotto

8 cups (64 fl oz/2 l) Vegetable Stock
  (page 12) or broth
3 tablespoons extra-virgin olive oil
2 shallots, finely chopped
2½ cups (17½ oz/545 g) Arborio rice
2 beets, trimmed, peeled, and coarsely
  shredded
1 cup (8 fl oz/250 ml) orange juice
salt and ground pepper to taste
6 oz (185 g) fresh goat cheese
2 tablespoons snipped fresh chives
2 tablespoons coarsely chopped flat-leaf
  (Italian) parsley
2 tablespoons grated orange zest

Just two beets, shredded raw and added toward the end of cooking, give the risotto an astonishing red color. Serve it with the goat cheese as a vegetarian main course. Or leave out the cheese and offer the risotto as an unusual accompaniment to grilled fish such as tuna or sea bass.

Pour the stock or broth into a saucepan and bring to a simmer. Adjust the heat to keep the liquid hot.

In a large, heavy saucepan over medium heat, warm the olive oil. Add the shallots and sauté until translucent, about 2 minutes. Add the rice and stir until white spots appear in the center of the grains, about 1 minute. Add a ladleful of the hot stock or broth, reduce the heat to maintain a simmer, and cook, stirring constantly, until the liquid is absorbed, about 2 minutes. Continue adding the liquid, a ladleful at a time and stirring constantly, until all of it is absorbed, 20–25 minutes longer.

Stir in the shredded beets and the orange juice. Continue cooking and stirring until the beets are heated through, the rice is just tender but slightly firm in the center, and the mixture is creamy, about 2 minutes. Season with salt and pepper.

To serve, spoon onto warmed individual plates and crumble the goat cheese evenly on top. Garnish with the chives, parsley, and orange zest.

Serves 6

Risotto Primavera

½ lb (250 g) asparagus

3½ cups (28 fl oz/875 ml) Vegetable Stock (*page 12*), Chicken Stock (*page 13*), or broth

2 tablespoons olive oil

1 yellow onion, thinly sliced

6 fresh mushrooms, brushed clean and thinly sliced

1¼ cups (9 oz/280 g) Arborio rice

½ cup (4 fl oz/125 ml) dry white wine

1 green or red bell pepper (capsicum), seeded and cut into long, narrow strips

1 yellow zucchini (courgette) or crookneck squash, trimmed, quartered lengthwise, and then thinly sliced crosswise

½ cup (2 oz/60 g) grated Parmesan cheese

salt and ground pepper to taste

This springtime risotto, with its healthful mix of fresh vegetables, needs only sliced tomatoes or a simple green salad and crusty bread to complete the meal.

Cut off the top 2 inches (5 cm) from each asparagus spear (save the bottoms for another use); cut on the diagonal into pieces ½ inch (12 mm) thick. Set aside.

Pour the stock or broth into a saucepan and bring to a simmer. Adjust the heat to keep the liquid hot.

In a large, heavy saucepan over medium-low heat, warm the olive oil. Add the onion and mushrooms and sauté, stirring, until softened, about 3 minutes. Add the rice and stir until white spots appear in the center of the grains, about 1 minute. Add the wine and stir until absorbed, about 2 minutes. Add a ladleful of the stock or broth, adjust the heat to maintain a simmer, and cook, stirring constantly, until the liquid is absorbed. Continue adding liquid, a ladleful at a time and stirring constantly, until the rice starts to soften, about 10 minutes.

Add the bell pepper and a ladleful of the liquid and cook, stirring constantly, until the liquid is absorbed. Add the squash and asparagus and another ladleful of the liquid and cook, stirring constantly, until the liquid is absorbed. Continue adding the liquid, a ladleful at a time and stirring constantly, until the rice is just tender but slightly firm in the center and the mixture is creamy. The total cooking time is 20–25 minutes.

Add the Parmesan cheese and season with salt and pepper. Stir to mix well.

Spoon into warmed individual bowls and serve.

Serves 4

Saffron Risotto with Crab

1 bunch small-leaved spinach, 4–5 oz
   (125–155 g)
2 cups (16 fl oz/500 ml) bottled clam
   juice
2 cups (16 fl oz/500 ml) water
½ teaspoon saffron threads
pinch of salt, plus salt to taste
¼ cup (2 oz/60 g) unsalted butter
1 small yellow onion, finely chopped
1½ cups (10½ oz/330 g) Arborio rice
1 cup (8 fl oz/250 ml) dry white wine
1 tablespoon dry Marsala wine
ground pepper to taste
½ lb (250 g) fresh-cooked crabmeat,
   picked over for any cartilage or shell
   fragments and flaked
2 tablespoons lemon juice
chopped fresh flat-leaf (Italian) parsley
   (optional)

*The flavors of saffron and crab blend particularly well with rich,
creamy risotto. If fresh-cooked crabmeat is unavailable, use medium-
sized shrimp (prawns), peeled and deveined, and cook them before
adding to the risotto.*

Rinse the spinach, drain well, and remove the stems. Pick out
about 30 of the smallest leaves; reserve the rest for another use.
Wrap the leaves in a damp kitchen towel and set aside.

Pour the clam juice and water into a saucepan and bring to a
simmer. Adjust the heat to keep the liquid hot.

Place the saffron threads and the pinch of salt in a large metal
spoon and hold over heat until warmed, just a few seconds. Using
a teaspoon, crush the saffron threads to a powder. Place in a small
bowl, add ½ cup (4 fl oz/125 ml) of the hot liquid, and set aside.

In a large, heavy saucepan over medium-low heat, melt the
butter. Add the onion and sauté until translucent, 4–5 minutes.
Add the rice and stir until white spots appear in the center of the
grains, about 1 minute. Add the white wine, adjust the heat to
maintain a simmer, and cook, stirring constantly, until absorbed,
3–4 minutes. Add the saffron broth and stir until absorbed, about
2 minutes longer. Add a ladleful of the liquid and stir constantly
until absorbed. Continue adding the liquid, a ladleful at a time
and stirring constantly, until the rice is just tender but slightly firm
in the center and the mixture is creamy, 20–25 minutes longer.

Stir in the Marsala and season with salt and pepper. Stir to mix
well. Then gently stir in the crab and finally the lemon juice.

To serve, arrange the spinach leaves in warmed individual
bowls. Spoon the risotto on the spinach and garnish with the
parsley, if desired.

Serves 4

Lobster and Champagne Risotto

2 teaspoons salt, plus salt to taste

2 live lobsters, about 1¼ lb (625 g) each

3 cups (24 fl oz/750 ml) dry champagne
or sparkling wine

3 tablespoons unsalted butter

1 large yellow onion, minced

1½ cups (10½ oz/330 g) Arborio rice

¼ cup (⅓ oz/10 g) snipped fresh chives,
plus whole chives for garnish

2 tablespoons chopped fresh flat-leaf
(Italian) parsley

½–1 teaspoon lemon juice

½ cup (4 fl oz/125 ml) heavy (double)
cream

ground pepper to taste

Fill a stockpot three-fourths full of water, add the 2 teaspoons salt, and bring to a boil. Add the lobsters, immersing completely, and cook until dark red, about 10 minutes. Using tongs, lift out the lobsters and let cool. Measure out 6 cups (48 fl oz/1.5 l) cooking liquid and return to the stockpot.

Make a small cut between the eyes of each lobster and hold by the tail over a sink to drain off excess cooking liquid. Place back side up on a work surface, insert a knife into the body at the point at which the tail and body sections meet, and cut lengthwise through the tail. Rotate the lobster and cut from the center through the head, cutting the lobster in half.

Reserve the tomalley (the liver) and any coral-colored roe for another use, or discard along with the black intestinal vein and any other organs. Remove the meat from the body, tail, and claws. Dice and set aside. Add the shells to the cooking liquid and reduce over high heat to 3 cups (24 fl oz/750 ml), about 15 minutes. Strain through a fine-mesh sieve lined with cheesecloth (muslin) into a saucepan; add the champagne or sparkling wine and bring to a simmer. Adjust the heat to keep the liquid hot.

In a large, heavy saucepan over medium heat, melt the butter. Add the onion and sauté until very soft, about 12 minutes. Add the rice and stir until white spots appear in the center of the grains. Add a ladleful of the liquid, adjust the heat to maintain a simmer, and cook, stirring constantly, until the liquid is absorbed. Continue adding the liquid, a ladleful at a time and stirring constantly, until the rice is just tender but slightly firm in the center and the mixture is creamy, 20–25 minutes longer. With the final ladleful of liquid, stir in the lobster meat, snipped chives, parsley, lemon juice, and cream. Season with salt and pepper.

Spoon into warmed individual bowls, garnish with whole chives, and serve.

Serves 6

Clams with Fresh Lemon Risotto

zest strips from 1½ lemons
6 cups (48 fl oz/1.5 l) Fish Stock
   (*page 13*) or 3 cups (24 fl oz/750 ml)
   each bottled clam juice and water
3 tablespoons vegetable oil
1 large yellow onion, chopped
2 cloves garlic, minced
60 small clams (about 4½ lb/2.25 kg),
   well scrubbed
3 cups (1⅓ lb/655 g) Arborio rice
¾ cup (6 fl oz/180 ml) dry white wine
3 large plum (Roma) tomatoes, seeded
   and chopped
½ cup (¾ oz/20 g) chopped fresh
   flat-leaf (Italian) parsley, plus sprigs
   for garnish
salt and ground pepper to taste

The rice absorbs the juices from the steamed clams, and the lemon zest further intensifies the flavor of this dish. Because your guests will be removing the clams from their shells at the table, be sure to provide extra napkins.

Bring a small saucepan three-fourths full of water to a boil. Add the lemon zest, boil for 30 seconds, and drain. Repeat the process, using fresh water.

Pour the stock or the clam juice and water into a saucepan and bring to a simmer. Adjust the heat to keep the liquid hot.

In a dutch oven or other large, heavy pot over medium-low heat, warm the vegetable oil. Add the onion and garlic and sauté until beginning to soften, about 5 minutes. Add the clams, discarding any that do not close to the touch, cover, and cook, shaking the pot occasionally, until the clams open, 5–10 minutes. Remove from the heat and, using tongs, transfer the clams to a bowl, discarding any that did not open. Cover and keep warm. If there is sand in the bottom of the pot, strain the liquid produced by the clams through a sieve lined with cheesecloth (muslin), then return the liquid to the pot.

Return the pot to medium heat, add the rice, and stir until white spots appear in the center of the grains, about 1 minute. Add the wine and stir until absorbed, about 2 minutes. Add the tomatoes and a ladleful of the hot liquid, adjust the heat to maintain a simmer, and cook, stirring constantly, until the liquid is absorbed. Continue adding the liquid, a ladleful at a time and stirring constantly, until the rice is just tender but slightly firm in the center and the mixture is creamy, 20–25 minutes.

Add the lemon zest and chopped parsley and season with salt and pepper. Stir to mix well.

To serve, spoon into warmed individual bowls and top with the clams, dividing evenly. Garnish with the parsley sprigs.

Serves 6

Risotto with Smoked Salmon, Spinach, and Goat Cheese

6 cups (48 fl oz/1.5 l) Fish Stock
  (*page 13*) or 3 cups (24 fl oz/750 ml)
  each bottled clam juice and water
3 tablespoons olive oil
2½ cups (17½ oz/545 g) Arborio rice
¾ cup (6 fl oz/180 ml) dry white wine
5 cups (10 oz/315 g) thinly sliced
  spinach leaves
1¼ cups (6½ oz/200 g) crumbled fresh
  goat cheese
¼ lb (125 g) smoked salmon, chopped
½ cup (¾ oz/20 g) snipped fresh chives
  or ½ cup (1½ oz/45 g) green (spring)
  onions, including tender green tops
salt and ground pepper to taste

The fresh flavors and colors make this a winning choice for brunch or lunch, accompanied with crusty rolls and dry white wine. Avoid salt-cured lox; it has an oily texture not suited to this dish.

Pour the stock or the clam juice and water into a saucepan and bring to a simmer. Adjust the heat to keep the liquid hot.

In a large, heavy saucepan over medium-low heat, warm the olive oil. Add the rice and stir until white spots appear in the center of the grains, about 1 minute. Add the wine and stir until absorbed, about 2 minutes. Add a ladleful of the liquid, adjust the heat to maintain a simmer, and cook, stirring constantly, until the liquid is absorbed. Continue adding the liquid, a ladleful at a time and stirring constantly, for 15 minutes.

Add the spinach and continue adding the liquid, a ladleful at a time and stirring constantly, until the rice is just tender but slightly firm in the center and the mixture is creamy, 5–10 minutes longer.

Add the goat cheese, smoked salmon, and chives or green onions and season with salt and pepper. Stir to mix well.

To serve, spoon onto warmed individual plates.

Serves 6

Smoked Trout Risotto

8 cups (64 fl oz/2 l) Vegetable Stock
(page 12) or broth
3 tablespoons extra-virgin olive oil
2 shallots, finely chopped
2½ cups (17½ oz/545 g) Arborio rice
½ cup (2 oz/60 g) grated Parmesan
cheese
¾ lb (375 g) smoked trout fillets,
separated into large flakes
1 small red (Spanish) onion, finely
chopped
¼ cup (1 oz/30 g) grated lemon zest
3 tablespoons small capers
ground pepper to taste
3 tablespoons snipped fresh chives
3 tablespoons finely chopped fresh
flat-leaf (Italian) parsley

Reminiscent of English kedgeree, a breakfast dish that features kippered herring, this risotto impresses with vivid flavors. Serve it for a light dinner or even as a brunch dish. Smoked trout fillets may be found in some delicatessens or well-stocked food stores. When carefully flaked, the fillets separate into individual V shapes, or chevrons; save 2 or 3 perfect ones to garnish each serving, if you like.

Pour the stock or broth into a saucepan and bring to a simmer. Adjust the heat to keep the liquid hot.

In a large, heavy saucepan over medium heat, warm the olive oil. Add the shallots and sauté until translucent, about 2 minutes. Add the rice and stir until white spots appear in the center of the grains, about 1 minute. Add a ladleful of the stock or broth, reduce the heat to maintain a simmer, and cook, stirring constantly, until the liquid is absorbed, about 2 minutes. Continue adding the liquid, a ladleful at a time and stirring constantly, until the rice is just tender but slightly firm in the center and the mixture is creamy, 20–25 minutes longer.

Add the Parmesan cheese and stir to mix well. Gently fold in the trout, onion, lemon zest, and capers. Season with pepper.

To serve, spoon onto warmed individual plates and garnish with the chives and parsley.

Serves 6

Asian Shrimp and Vegetable Risotto

8½ cups (68 fl oz/2.1 l) Chicken Stock
   (*page 13*) or broth
6 slices peeled fresh ginger
4 tablespoons (2 fl oz/60 ml) soy sauce
6 tablespoons (3 fl oz/90 ml) vegetable
   oil
2 cloves garlic, minced
2½ cups (17½ oz/545 g) Arborio rice
1 tablespoon cornstarch (cornflour)
1½ lb (750 g) shrimp (prawns), peeled
   and deveined
½ cup (2½ oz/75 g) slivered blanched
   almonds
½ lb (250 g) snow peas (mangetouts),
   trimmed
½ lb (250 g) baby bok choy, larger leaves
   halved, small leaves left whole
1 red bell pepper (capsicum), quartered,
   seeded, and the quarters cut crosswise
   into strips ¼ inch (6 mm) wide
2 green (spring) onions, including tender
   green tops, thinly sliced

*P*our 8 cups (64 fl oz/2 l) of the stock or broth into a saucepan. Add the ginger and 2 tablespoons of the soy sauce and bring to a boil. Adjust the heat to keep the liquid hot.

In a large, heavy saucepan over medium heat, warm 3 tablespoons of the vegetable oil. Add the garlic and sauté just until aromatic, about 1 minute. Add the rice and stir until white spots appear in the center of the grains, about 1 minute. Add a ladleful of the stock or broth, adjust the heat as necessary to maintain a simmer, and cook, stirring constantly, until the liquid is absorbed, about 2 minutes. Continue adding the liquid, a ladleful at a time and stirring constantly, until the rice is tender but slightly firm in the center and the mixture is creamy, 20–25 minutes longer. Remove from the heat, cover, and keep warm.

In a small cup, dissolve the cornstarch in the remaining ½ cup (4 fl oz/100 ml) stock or broth. In a wok or large frying pan over medium-high heat, warm the remaining 3 tablespoons vegetable oil and swirl the wok or pan to coat evenly. Add the shrimp and almonds and toss and stir until the shrimp turn uniformly bright pink, about 2 minutes. Using a slotted spoon, transfer to a bowl. Add the snow peas, bok choy, and bell pepper to the wok or pan and toss and stir until heated through but still crisp, 2–3 minutes. Add the shrimp, almonds, cornstarch mixture, and remaining 2 tablespoons soy sauce. Toss and stir until the shrimp and vegetables are lightly coated with sauce, about 1 minute longer.

Gently fold about half of the shrimp-vegetable mixture into the risotto. Spoon onto a warmed platter. Spoon the remaining shrimp-vegetable mixture on top. Garnish with the green onions and serve.

Serves 6

59

Scallop and Orange Zest Risotto

7 cups (56 fl oz/1.75 l) Fish Stock
  (*page 13*) or 3½ cups (28 fl oz/875 ml)
  each bottled clam juice and water
3 tablespoons unsalted butter
3 tablespoons vegetable oil
2 shallots, minced
2½ cups (17½ oz/545 g) Arborio rice
1 cup (8 fl oz/250 ml) dry white wine
1 red bell pepper (capsicum), roasted
  (*see glossary, page 104*) and cut into
  strips 1 inch (2.5 cm) long and ¼ inch
  (6 mm) wide
narrow zest strips from 1 orange
6 tablespoons (½ oz/15 g) snipped fresh
  chives
salt and ground white pepper to taste
1¼ lb (625 g) sea scallops

Risotto cooked with seafood broth and scented with orange zest makes a backdrop for plump, quickly seared sea scallops. You could also use small bay scallops; quickly sauté them, then fold into the rice.

*P*our the stock or the clam juice and water into a saucepan and bring to a gentle simmer. Adjust the heat to keep the liquid hot.

In a large, heavy saucepan over medium heat, melt 1 tablespoon of the butter with 1 tablespoon of the vegetable oil. Add the shallots and sauté just until they begin to turn translucent, 2–3 minutes. Add the rice and stir until white spots appear in the center of the grains, about 1 minute. Add the wine and stir until absorbed, about 2 minutes. Add a ladleful of the liquid, adjust the heat to maintain a bare simmer, and cook, stirring constantly until absorbed. Continue adding the liquid, a ladleful at a time and stirring constantly, until the rice is just tender but slightly firm in the center and the mixture is creamy, about 25 minutes longer. Reserve one ladleful of liquid. Stir in the bell pepper, orange zest, and 3 tablespoons of the chives and season with salt and white pepper. Remove from the heat, cover, and keep warm.

Rinse the scallops and pat dry, then season lightly with salt and pepper (take care not to oversalt, as some scallops may be salty). In a frying pan large enough to hold the scallops in a single layer, melt the remaining 2 tablespoons butter with the remaining 2 tablespoons vegetable oil over high heat. When the butter foams, add the scallops and cook, turning once, until golden, 1–2 minutes on each side.

Add the remaining ladleful of liquid to the risotto and stir until absorbed. Spoon the risotto onto warmed individual plates. Top the risotto with the scallops, garnish with the remaining 3 tablespoons chives, and serve.

Serves 6

Corn Risotto with Green Chiles and Shrimp

18 ears of corn, husks and silk removed

10 tablespoons (5 oz/150 g) unsalted butter

1 yellow onion, finely chopped

2 cups (16 fl oz/500 ml) Vegetable Stock (*page 12*), Chicken Stock (*page 13*), or broth

½ cup (4 oz/125 g) canned diced mild green chiles

2 tablespoons lime juice

salt and ground pepper to taste

1½ lb (750 g) shrimp (prawns), peeled and deveined

1½ teaspoons mild or hot pure red chili powder

1 avocado

3 tablespoons coarsely chopped fresh cilantro (fresh coriander)

This corn "risotto" is very much like old-fashioned creamed corn. The natural starches in fresh corn form a creamy sauce similar to the consistency of risotto, without the addition of cream. If you like, add 1 or 2 minced garlic cloves to the butter in which you sauté the shrimp.

Remove the kernels from 6 ears of corn: Hold each ear by its pointed end, steadying its stalk end on a cutting board. Using a sharp knife, cut down along the cob to strip off the kernels, turning the cob with each cut. Place the kernels in a bowl. Holding a box grater over the bowl and using the largest shredding holes, carefully grate the kernels off the remaining 12 ears.

In a large saucepan over medium heat, melt 6 tablespoons (3 oz/90 g) of the butter. Add the onion and sauté until translucent, 3–5 minutes. Stir in the corn, stock or broth, and green chiles, reduce the heat to low, and cook, stirring occasionally, until the mixture is thick and the corn is tender, about 10 minutes. Stir in the lime juice, season with salt and pepper, cover, and keep warm.

Dust the shrimp evenly with the chili powder and a little salt. In a large frying pan over high heat, melt the remaining 4 tablespoons (2 oz/60 g) butter. As soon as the butter foams, add the shrimp and sauté until they turn bright pink, about 4 minutes. Remove from the heat.

Spoon the corn risotto onto warmed individual plates. Arrange the shrimp on top. Cut the avocado in half lengthwise and remove the pit and peel. Cut each half lengthwise into 6 equal wedges. Arrange 2 avocado wedges on each plate, garnish with the cilantro, and serve.

Serves 6

Risotto with Veal Tenderloin and Balsamic Vinegar Glaze

4 plum (Roma) tomatoes, peeled, seeded, and chopped

3 tablespoons shredded fresh basil

salt and ground white pepper to taste

7 cups (56 fl oz/1.75 l) beef broth

1 fresh rosemary sprig

6 tablespoons (3 fl oz/90 ml) extra-virgin olive oil

2 shallots, minced

2½ cups (17½ oz/545 g) Arborio rice

1 cup (8 fl oz/250 ml) dry white wine

1½ lb (750 g) veal tenderloin, well trimmed

6 tablespoons (3 fl oz/90 ml) balsamic vinegar

In a small bowl, toss together the tomatoes and basil. Season with salt and white pepper and set aside.

Pour the broth into a saucepan, add the rosemary sprig, and bring to a simmer. Adjust the heat to keep the liquid hot.

In a large, heavy saucepan over medium heat, warm 3 tablespoons of the olive oil. Add the shallots and sauté for 2–3 minutes. Add the rice and stir until white spots appear in the center of the grains, about 1 minute. Add the wine and stir until absorbed. Add a ladleful of the broth, reduce the heat to maintain a simmer, and cook, stirring constantly, until the broth is absorbed. Continue adding the broth, a ladleful at a time and stirring constantly, until the rice is just tender but slightly firm in the center and the mixture is creamy, 20–25 minutes longer. Leave the rosemary sprig in the pan when scooping up the final ladleful.

About halfway through the cooking of the risotto, season the veal generously with salt and white pepper. In a frying pan over medium-high heat, warm the remaining 3 tablespoons olive oil. Add the veal and cook, turning occasionally, until evenly seared golden brown, 4–5 minutes total. Reduce the heat to medium-low and continue cooking until done to your liking, 5–7 minutes longer for medium. Transfer to a cutting board. Pour off most of the fat from the pan, return it to high heat, add the vinegar, and deglaze the pan, stirring to dislodge any browned bits from the pan bottom. Remove from the heat and set aside.

Season the risotto with salt and white pepper and spoon onto warmed individual plates. Cut the veal tenderloin crosswise into thin slices and arrange on top of the risotto. Drizzle the balsamic vinegar glaze over the veal slices. Place a heaping spoonful of the tomato-basil mixture on top of each serving.

Serves 6

Risotto with Vegetable Streamers and Pancetta

8 cups (64 fl oz/2 l) Vegetable Stock
  (page 12) or broth
3 tablespoons extra-virgin olive oil
1 small yellow onion, finely chopped
¼ lb (125 g) thinly sliced pancetta, diced
2½ cups (17½ oz/545 g) Arborio rice
1 red bell pepper (capsicum), seeded
  and cut lengthwise into long, very
  narrow strips
1 carrot, peeled and cut into long,
  narrow shreds
1 yellow summer squash, trimmed and
  cut into long, narrow shreds
1 zucchini (courgette), trimmed and cut
  into long, narrow shreds
¾ cup (3 oz/90 g) grated Parmesan
  cheese
ground pepper to taste
3 tablespoons snipped fresh chives

You can transform this colorful risotto into a vegetarian dish by omitting the pancetta. Either way, serve it as a casual main course, or stretch it to 8 servings as a side dish.

Pour the stock or broth into a saucepan and bring to a simmer. Adjust the heat to keep the liquid hot.

In a large, heavy saucepan over medium heat, warm the olive oil. Add the onion and pancetta and sauté, stirring frequently, until the onion turns translucent and the pancetta looks frizzled, about 5 minutes. Add the rice and stir until white spots appear in the center of the grains, about 1 minute. Add a ladleful of the stock or broth, adjust the heat to maintain a bare simmer, and cook, stirring constantly, until the liquid is absorbed. Continue adding the liquid, a ladleful at a time and stirring constantly, until the rice is just tender but slightly firm in the center, 20–25 minutes longer. When you add the final ladleful of liquid, stir in the bell pepper, carrot, yellow squash, and zucchini so they heat through.

Add the cheese and season with pepper. Stir to mix well.

To serve, spoon into warmed individual bowls and garnish with the chives.

Serves 6

Turkey Risotto

6 cups (48 fl oz/1.5 l) Chicken Stock
  (*page 13*) or broth
2 tablespoons olive oil or unsalted butter
½ cup (2½ oz/75 g) minced yellow onion
1½ cups (10½ oz/330 g) Arborio rice
2 cups (12 oz/375 g) diced, cooked
  turkey (1-inch/2.5-cm dice)
1 teaspoon chopped fresh sage or
  2 teaspoons chopped fresh thyme
1 cup (5 oz/155 g) shelled fresh or
  thawed frozen English peas (optional)
¼ cup (1½ oz/45 g) finely diced
  prosciutto (optional)
⅓ cup (1½ oz/45 g) finely diced fontina
  cheese or ¼ cup (1 oz/30 g) grated
  Parmesan cheese
salt and ground pepper to taste
minced fresh flat-leaf (Italian) parsley

Turkey left over from a holiday dinner can be turned into this delicious risotto. If you still have the carcass on hand, make stock with it and use in place of the Chicken Stock called for here.

*P*our the stock or broth into a saucepan and bring to a simmer. Adjust the heat to keep the liquid hot.

In a large, heavy saucepan over medium heat, warm the olive oil or melt the butter. Add the onion and sauté until soft, 8–10 minutes. Add the rice and stir until white spots appear in the center of the grains, about 1 minute. Add a ladleful of the stock or broth, adjust the heat to maintain a simmer, and cook, stirring constantly, until the liquid is absorbed, about 2 minutes. Continue adding the liquid, a ladleful at a time and stirring constantly, until the rice is just tender but slightly firm in the center and the mixture is creamy, 20–25 minutes longer. When you add the final ladleful of liquid, stir in the turkey and sage or thyme, and the peas and prosciutto, if using. Add the fontina cheese, if using, and season with salt and pepper. Stir until well mixed.

To serve, spoon into warmed individual bowls and, if you have not added the fontina cheese, sprinkle with the Parmesan cheese. Garnish with the parsley.

Serves 4

Risotto with Chicken, Roasted Peppers, and Peas

7 cups (56 fl oz/1.75 l) Chicken Stock
  (*page 13*) or broth
½ teaspoon saffron threads
1¼ lb (625 g) boneless, skinless chicken,
  cut into strips about ½ inch
  (12 mm) wide
salt and ground pepper to taste
6 tablespoons (3 fl oz/90 ml) extra-virgin
  olive oil
1 yellow onion, chopped
3 cloves garlic, minced
½ teaspoon red pepper flakes
2½ cups (17½ oz/545 g) Arborio rice
1 cup (8 fl oz/250 ml) dry white wine
1½ teaspoons dried rosemary
1 red bell pepper (capsicum), roasted
  (*see glossary, page 104*) and cut into
  strips 1 inch (2.5 cm) long and ¼ inch
  (6 mm) wide
1½ cups (8 oz/250 g) thawed frozen
  petite peas
3 tablespoons finely chopped fresh
  flat-leaf (Italian) parsley

Here, risotto is turned into a Spanish main course, in the style of arroz con pollo. *For an even more robust version, add some spicy chorizo sausage, removed from the casing and sautéed in small chunks, after the chicken has been cooked.*

*P*our the stock or broth into a saucepan, add the saffron, and bring to a gentle simmer. Adjust the heat to keep the liquid hot.

Season the chicken with salt and pepper. In a large, heavy saucepan over medium-high heat, warm 3 tablespoons of the olive oil. Working in batches, add the chicken to the pan and sauté, turning frequently, until light golden brown, 3–4 minutes. Transfer to a plate and set aside.

In the same pan over medium heat, warm the remaining 3 tablespoons olive oil. Add the onion and garlic and sauté, stirring, until they begin to color slightly, 3–4 minutes. Stir in the red pepper flakes and sauté for about 1 minute longer.

Add the rice and stir until white spots appear in the center of the grains, about 1 minute. Add the wine and rosemary and stir until the wine is absorbed, about 2 minutes. Add a ladleful of the stock or broth, adjust the heat to maintain a simmer, and cook, stirring constantly, until the liquid is absorbed. Continue adding the liquid, a ladleful at a time and stirring constantly, until the rice is just tender but slightly firm in the center and the mixture is creamy, 20–25 minutes. When you add the final few ladlefuls of liquid, stir in the chicken, bell pepper, and peas. Taste and adjust the seasonings with salt and pepper.

To serve, spoon into warmed individual bowls and garnish with the parsley.

Serves 6

Beef Bolognese Layered with Classic Risotto

¼ cup (2 oz/60 g) unsalted butter
¼ lb (125 g) pancetta or bacon, chopped
2 large yellow onions, chopped
2 large carrots, peeled and chopped
1½ lb (750 g) ground (minced) lean beef
1 cup (8 fl oz/250 ml) dry red wine
2 cups (16 fl oz/500 ml) beef broth
1½ cups (12 fl oz/375 ml) milk
8 large plum (Roma) tomatoes, peeled,
    seeded, and chopped, or 1 can
    (28 oz/875 g) plum (Roma) tomatoes
    with juice
1 cup (8 fl oz/250 ml) tomato juice, if
    using fresh tomatoes
salt and ground pepper to taste
Classic Risotto (page 7)
½ cup (2 oz/60 g) grated Parmesan
    cheese, plus additional cheese
    for serving

The bolognese sauce ordinarily served over spaghetti complements risotto in this easy recipe. For a lighter version, eliminate the pancetta, halve the butter, and substitute ground turkey for the beef.

In a large, heavy saucepan over medium heat, melt the butter. Add the pancetta or bacon, onions, and carrots and sauté until the mixture begins to brown, about 10 minutes. Add the beef and cook, breaking up the meat with a fork, until browned, about 5 minutes.

Add the wine, reduce the heat to medium-low, and simmer, stirring constantly, until the wine is absorbed, about 5 minutes. Add the broth and simmer, stirring occasionally, until almost absorbed, about 15 minutes. Add the milk and simmer until almost evaporated, about 15 minutes.

Add the fresh tomatoes and tomato juice or the canned tomatoes with their juice, reduce the heat to low, and simmer gently, uncovered, stirring occasionally, until very thick, about 1½ hours. Season with salt and pepper.

To serve, spoon half of the risotto into a warmed large, shallow serving bowl. Top with half of the beef mixture and sprinkle with ¼ cup (1 oz/30 g) of the Parmesan cheese. Repeat the layers. Pass the additional cheese at the table.

Serves 4

Coconut Risotto with Pork Saté

FOR THE PORK SATÉ:

1 cup (8 fl oz/250 ml) coconut milk

6 tablespoons (3 oz/90 g) chunky peanut
   butter

2 tablespoons soy sauce

1½ tablespoons honey

1½ tablespoons lemon juice

2–3 teaspoons chili paste

1½ lb (750 g) boneless pork loin chops,
   trimmed and cut lengthwise into strips
   about ¼ inch (6 mm) wide

FOR THE COCONUT RISOTTO:

4¼ cups (34 fl oz/1.1 l) Chicken Stock
   (*page 13*) or broth

3½ cups (28 fl oz/875 ml) coconut milk

2 tablespoons vegetable oil

2 shallots, finely chopped

2½ cups (17½ oz/545 g) Arborio rice

salt and ground white pepper to taste

3 tablespoons coarsely chopped fresh
   cilantro (fresh coriander)

*Serve the risotto and pork as a main course or offer the risotto alone
with other Asian-style grilled meat, poultry, or seafood.*

If using wooden skewers for the pork saté, soak in water to cover
for about 20 minutes.

In a bowl, stir together the coconut milk, peanut butter, soy
sauce, honey, lemon juice, and chili paste. Place the pork strips in
another bowl, pour about one-third of the peanut sauce over the
strips, and turn to coat evenly. Set the remaining sauce aside.
Drain the skewers, then thread the pork onto the skewers. Place
in a shallow nonaluminum dish, cover, and refrigerate.

To make the risotto, pour the stock or broth and the coconut
milk into a saucepan and bring to simmer. Adjust the heat to keep
the liquid hot.

In a large, heavy saucepan over medium heat, warm the
vegetable oil. Add the shallots and sauté until golden brown,
3–4 minutes. Add the rice and stir until white spots appear in the
center of the grains, about 1 minute. Add a ladleful of the hot
liquid, adjust the heat to maintain a simmer, and cook, stirring
constantly, until the liquid is absorbed. Continue adding the
liquid, a ladleful at a time and stirring constantly, until the rice is
tender but slightly firm in the center and the mixture is creamy,
20–25 minutes longer. Season with salt and white pepper.

About 10 minutes before the risotto is done, preheat a broiler
(griller). Place the skewers on a broiler pan and slip under the
broiler. Broil (grill), turning once, until the pork is golden brown,
about 3 minutes on each side.

Spoon the risotto onto heated individual plates. Arrange the
skewers on top. Drizzle with the reserved peanut sauce, garnish
with the cilantro, and serve.

Serves 6

Porcini Mushroom and Spicy Sausage Risotto

1½ oz (45 g) dried porcini mushrooms

3 cups (24 fl oz/750 ml) hot water

2½ cups (20 fl oz/625 ml) Chicken Stock (*page 13*) or broth

1 tablespoon olive oil

1 large yellow onion, chopped

½ lb (250 g) fresh spicy Italian sausages, casings removed

¾ lb (375 g) button mushrooms, brushed clean and sliced

1½ teaspoons finely chopped fresh rosemary

2½ cups (17½ oz/545 g) Arborio rice

¾ cup (6 fl oz/180 ml) dry white wine

1 bay leaf

⅓ cup (3 fl oz/80 ml) half-and-half (half cream)

2 cups (8 oz/250 g) grated Parmesan cheese

salt and ground pepper to taste

If you prefer a milder dish, substitute sweet Italian sausage for the spicy variety as the porcini mushrooms provide plenty of flavor.

In a small bowl, combine the porcini mushrooms and the hot water. Let stand for 30 minutes to soften. Using a slotted spoon, remove the mushrooms from the soaking liquid. Chop the mushrooms and set aside. Line a sieve with cheesecloth (muslin) and pour the liquid through it into a saucepan.

Add the stock or broth to the mushroom soaking liquid and bring to a simmer. Adjust the heat to keep the liquid hot.

In a large, heavy saucepan over medium heat, warm the olive oil. Add the onion and sauté until it begins to soften, about 5 minutes. Add the sausage meat, increase the heat to high, and cook, breaking up the meat with a fork, just until it is no longer pink, about 6 minutes. Add the button mushrooms and rosemary and stir until the mushrooms begin to soften, about 5 minutes.

Reduce the heat to medium, add the porcini mushrooms and the rice, and stir until white spots appear in the center of the grains, about 1 minute. Add the wine and bay leaf and stir until the wine is absorbed, about 2 minutes. Add a ladleful of the stock or broth, reduce the heat to maintain a simmer, and cook, stirring constantly, until the liquid is absorbed. Continue adding the liquid, a ladleful at a time and stirring constantly, until the rice is just tender but slightly firm in the center and the mixture is creamy, 20–25 minutes longer.

Remove the bay leaf and discard. Add the half-and-half and Parmesan cheese and season with salt and pepper. Stir to mix well.

Spoon onto warmed individual plates and serve.

Serves 6

Ham, Pea, and Parmesan Risotto

6 cups (48 fl oz/1.5 l) Chicken Stock
(*page 13*) or broth
2 tablespoons unsalted butter
1 yellow onion, chopped
¾ lb (375 g) ham, cut into ½-inch
(12-mm) pieces
2½ cups (17½ oz/545 g) Arborio rice
2 cups (10 oz/315 g) shelled fresh or
thawed frozen English peas
1 cup (4 oz/125 g) grated Parmesan
cheese
1 tablespoon finely chopped fresh thyme,
plus sprigs for garnish
salt and ground pepper to taste

Inspired by the classic pasta dish fettuccine Alfredo, this creamy risotto is especially satisfying on a cold winter's night. For a vegetarian version, leave out the ham and substitute Vegetable Stock (page 12) for the Chicken Stock.

Pour the stock or broth into a saucepan and bring to a simmer. Adjust the heat to keep the liquid hot.

In a large, heavy saucepan over medium-low heat, melt the butter. Add the onion and sauté until beginning to soften, about 5 minutes. Add the ham and sauté until the onion is tender, about 5 minutes longer. Add the rice and stir until white spots appear in the center of the grains, about 1 minute. Add a ladleful of the stock or broth, adjust the heat to maintain a simmer, and cook, stirring constantly, until the liquid is absorbed, about 2 minutes. Continue adding the liquid, a ladleful at a time and stirring constantly, until the rice starts to soften, about 10 minutes.

Add the peas and continue adding the liquid, a ladleful at a time and stirring constantly, until the rice is just tender but slightly firm in the center and the mixture is creamy, about 10–15 minutes longer.

Add the Parmesan cheese and chopped thyme and season with salt and pepper. Stir to mix well.

To serve, spoon into warmed individual bowls and garnish with the thyme sprigs.

Serves 6

Prosciutto and Radicchio Risotto

5½ cups (44 fl oz/1.35 l) Chicken Stock
(page 13), Vegetable Stock (page 12),
or broth
2 tablespoons olive oil
½ large yellow onion, chopped
2 cups (14 oz/440 g) Arborio rice
¾ cup (6 fl oz/180 ml) dry white wine
2 heads radicchio, 4–5 oz (125–155 g)
each, thinly sliced
3 oz (90 g) thinly sliced prosciutto,
coarsely chopped
¾ cup (3 oz/90 g) grated Parmesan
cheese, plus additional cheese
for serving
salt and ground pepper to taste

*The pairing of two classic Italian ingredients makes this dish both
simple and elegant, a perfect companion to grilled or broiled lamb. If
you cannot find prosciutto, substitute another air-cured raw ham.*

Pour the stock or broth into a saucepan and bring to a simmer.
Adjust the heat to keep the liquid hot.

In a large, heavy saucepan over medium-low heat, warm the
olive oil. Add the onion and sauté until translucent, about
8 minutes. Add the rice and stir until white spots appear in the
center of the grains, about 1 minute. Add the wine and stir until
absorbed, about 2 minutes. Add a ladleful of the stock or broth,
adjust the heat to maintain a simmer, and cook, stirring constantly, until the liquid is absorbed. Continue adding the liquid, a
ladleful at a time and stirring constantly, until the rice starts to
soften, about 10 minutes.

Add the radicchio and continue adding the liquid, a ladleful
at a time and stirring constantly, until the rice is just tender
but slightly firm in the center and the mixture is creamy,
10–15 minutes longer.

Add the prosciutto and the ¾ cup (3 oz/90 g) Parmesan cheese
and season with salt and pepper. Stir to mix well.

To serve, spoon onto a platter. Pass the additional cheese at
the table.

Serves 4

Roast Chicken and Kale Risotto

7 cups (56 fl oz/1.75 l) Chicken Stock
  (*page 13*) or broth
1 bunch leafy kale, about ½ lb (250 g),
  coarse stems removed and leaves
  cut crosswise into strips 1 inch
  (2.5 cm) wide
¼ cup (2 fl oz/60 ml) extra-virgin
  olive oil
1 yellow onion, chopped
2½ cups (17½ oz/545 g) Arborio rice
1 cup (8 fl oz/250 ml) dry white wine
2 cups (12 oz/375 g) torn cooked
  chicken meat (bite-sized pieces)
2 tablespoons lemon juice
1 cup (4 oz/125 g) grated pecorino
  romano cheese
ground pepper to taste

Comfortingly homestyle, this risotto gains appeal from the strips of kale, which retain a satisfying edge of crunch and chewiness even after being wilted and then simmered with the rice. If you don't have leftover roast chicken on hand, this recipe is well worth the purchase of an already roasted chicken.

*P*our the stock or broth into a saucepan and bring to a simmer. Adjust the heat to keep the liquid hot.

Meanwhile, rinse the kale thoroughly and place in a saucepan with the rinse water still clinging to the leaves. Cover and place over medium heat just until the leaves begin to wilt, 1–2 minutes. Drain well, pressing any liquid from the leaves, and set aside.

In a large, heavy saucepan over medium heat, warm the olive oil. Add the onion and sauté until it begins to turn golden brown, 10–12 minutes. Add the rice and stir until white spots appear at the center of the grains, about 1 minute. Add the wine and stir until absorbed, about 2 minutes. Add a ladleful of the stock or broth, reduce the heat to maintain a simmer, and cook, stirring constantly, until the liquid is absorbed. Continue adding the liquid, a ladleful at a time and stirring constantly, until the rice begins to soften, about 10 minutes.

Stir in the wilted kale and continue adding the liquid, a ladleful at a time and stirring constantly, until the rice is just tender but slightly firm in the center and the mixture is creamy, 10–15 minutes longer. About 4 minutes before the rice is done, add the chicken pieces and the lemon juice, allowing sufficient time for the chicken to heat through as the rice finishes cooking.

Add the pecorino romano cheese and season generously with pepper. Stir to mix well.

Spoon into warmed individual bowls and serve.

Serves 6

Osso Buco on a Bed of Risotto

2 tablespoons unsalted butter

1½ large yellow onions, chopped

2 cloves garlic, minced

narrow zest strips from 2 lemons

2 teaspoons finely chopped fresh
   rosemary

2 bay leaves

1 teaspoon dried sage

2 tablespoons olive oil

6 center-cut veal shanks, about ¾ lb
   (375 g) each

salt and ground pepper to taste

1 cup (5 oz/155 g) all-purpose (plain)
   flour

1 cup (8 fl oz/250 ml) dry white wine

2½ cups (20 fl oz/625 ml) Chicken Stock
   (*page 13*) or broth, or as needed

⅓ cup (½ oz/15 g) finely chopped fresh
   flat-leaf (Italian) parsley

1 tablespoon grated lemon zest

Classic Risotto (*page 7*)

Slow simmering gives veal shanks rich, deep flavor, highlighted here by lemon zest and fresh rosemary.

*P*reheat an oven to 375°F (190°C).

In a dutch oven or other large, heavy pot over medium heat, melt the butter. Add the onions and sauté until translucent, about 8 minutes. Add half of the garlic, half of the lemon zest strips, and the rosemary, bay leaves, and sage and sauté until the garlic is translucent, about 3 minutes. Remove from the heat.

In a large, heavy frying pan over medium-high heat, warm the olive oil. Working in batches, season the veal with salt and pepper, coat with flour (shake off excess), add to the pan, and cook, turning once, until browned, about 4 minutes on each side. Place the veal on top of the onions in the dutch oven.

Pour off and discard the drippings from the frying pan. Raise the heat to high, add the wine, bring to a boil, and deglaze the pan, stirring with a wooden spoon to dislodge any browned bits from the pan bottom. Add the wine mixture to the dutch oven.

Add enough stock or broth to come to the top of the veal and bring to a boil. Cover and place in the oven. Bake, turning the veal and stirring occasionally, until the meat is tender and the sauce is creamy, about 1½ hours.

In a small bowl, stir together the parsley, grated lemon zest, and remaining garlic.

To serve, season the veal sauce with salt and pepper. Spoon the risotto onto warmed individual plates. Top with the veal and sauce and sprinkle with the parsley mixture. Garnish with the remaining lemon zest strips.

Serves 6

Chicken and Artichoke Risotto

juice of 1½ lemons

6 artichokes

7 cups (56 fl oz/1.75 l) Chicken Stock
(*page 13*) or broth

6 tablespoons (3 fl oz/90 ml) extra-virgin
olive oil

salt and ground pepper to taste

1 lb (500 g) boneless, skinless chicken
breasts, cut on the diagonal into strips
about ½ inch (12 mm) wide

3 cloves garlic, minced

2 shallots, chopped

2½ cups (17½ oz/545 g) Arborio rice

1 cup (8 fl oz/250 ml) dry white wine

1½ teaspoons dried oregano

½ cup (2 oz/60 g) grated Parmesan
cheese, plus 2 oz (60 g) Parmesan
cheese cut into shavings (optional)

2 tablespoons coarsely chopped fresh
flat-leaf (Italian) parsley

2 tablespoons finely shredded fresh basil

*H*ave ready a bowl of water to which you have added the juice of ½ lemon. Remove the tough outer leaves of the artichokes. Trim off the stems and top one-third of the leaves. Cut in half lengthwise, then scoop out the prickly chokes. Cut lengthwise into thin wedges and place in the bowl of lemon water.

Pour the stock or broth into a saucepan and bring to a gentle simmer. Adjust the heat to keep the liquid hot.

In a large frying pan over high heat, warm 3 tablespoons of the olive oil. Drain the artichokes, add to the pan, season lightly with salt and pepper, and sauté until lightly golden. Transfer to a bowl. Season the chicken with salt and pepper, add to the pan, and sauté until light golden brown, 4–5 minutes. Transfer to the bowl with the artichokes. Add the juice of 1 lemon to the pan and deglaze the pan, stirring with a wooden spoon to dislodge any browned bits from the pan bottom. Pour over the chicken and artichokes.

In a large, heavy saucepan over medium heat, warm the remaining 3 tablespoons olive oil. Add the garlic and shallots and sauté until they begin to turn translucent, 2–3 minutes. Add the rice and stir until white spots appear in the center of the grains, about 1 minute. Add the wine and oregano and stir until the wine is absorbed. Add a ladleful of the stock or broth, adjust the heat to maintain a simmer, and cook, stirring constantly, until absorbed. Continue adding the liquid, a ladleful at a time and stirring constantly, until the rice is just tender but slightly firm in the center and the mixture is creamy, 20–25 minutes longer. When you add the final few ladlefuls of liquid, stir in the chicken and artichokes.

Stir in the grated Parmesan cheese. Taste and adjust the seasonings with salt and pepper.

To serve, spoon into warmed individual bowls. Garnish with the shaved Parmesan, if desired, and the parsley and basil.

Serves 6

Fennel, Leek, and Pancetta Risotto

1 fennel bulb

5 cups (40 fl oz/1.25 l) Chicken Stock
(page 13), Vegetable Stock (page 12),
or broth

2 tablespoons olive oil

2 leeks, white parts and 1½ inches
(4 cm) of the green, halved lengthwise
and sliced crosswise

1½ cups (10½ oz/330 g) Arborio rice

¼ lb (125 g) pancetta, chopped

½ teaspoon fennel seeds, crushed

¾ cup (6 fl oz/180 ml) dry white wine

½ cup (2 oz/60 g) grated pecorino
romano cheese, plus additional cheese
for serving

salt and ground pepper to taste

Three forms of fennel—the bulb vegetable, the dried seeds, and the feathery fronds—add the subtly sweet flavor of anise to this risotto. If you can't find pancetta, substitute another kind of bacon.

Cut off the stems and feathery tops and any bruised outer stalks from the fennel bulb. Reserve the fronds for garnish. Quarter the bulb lengthwise and then thinly slice crosswise. Set aside.

Pour the stock or broth into a saucepan and bring to a simmer. Adjust the heat to keep the liquid hot.

In a large, heavy saucepan over low heat, warm the olive oil. Add the leeks and sauté until they begin to soften, about 5 minutes. Add the sliced fennel and sauté until the fennel begins to soften, about 5 minutes. Add the rice, pancetta, and fennel seeds and stir until white spots appear in the center of the grains, about 1 minute. Add the wine and stir until absorbed, about 2 minutes. Add a ladleful of the stock or broth, adjust the heat to maintain a simmer, and cook, stirring constantly, until the liquid is absorbed. Continue adding the liquid, a ladleful at a time and stirring constantly, until the rice is just tender but slightly firm in the center and the mixture is creamy, 20–25 minutes longer.

Add the ½ cup (2 oz/60 g) pecorino romano cheese and season with salt and pepper. Stir to mix well.

To serve, spoon onto warmed individual plates and garnish with tiny fennel fronds. Pass the additional cheese at the table.

Serves 4

Barley Risotto with Greek Lamb Ragout

Lamb and barley, time-honored companions, form the basis of this robust main course. If you like, substitute boneless chicken breast for the lamb and cook the barley in Chicken Stock (page 13).

FOR THE BARLEY RISOTTO:

6½ cups (52 fl oz/1.6 l) beef broth

1 large fresh oregano sprig

3 tablespoons extra-virgin olive oil

3 cloves garlic, minced

2¼ cups (15 oz/470 g) pearl barley

FOR THE LAMB RAGOUT:

2¼ lb (1.1 kg) well-trimmed boneless
 lamb loin, cut into ½–¾-inch
 (12-mm–2-cm) chunks

salt and ground pepper to taste

⅓ cup (3 fl oz/80 ml) extra-virgin olive
 oil

2 yellow onions, coarsely chopped

1½ lb (750 g) tomatoes, coarsely
 chopped

1½ tablespoons dried oregano

1½ teaspoons sugar

1 cup (5 oz/155 g) pitted Kalamata
 olives, halved

6 oz (185 g) feta cheese, crumbled

6 tablespoons (½ oz/15 g) finely
 shredded fresh basil leaves

*T*o make the barley risotto, pour the broth into a saucepan, add the oregano sprig, and bring to a boil. Remove from the heat.

In a large, heavy saucepan over medium-low heat, warm the olive oil with the garlic just until the garlic gives off its aroma, 1–2 minutes. Add the barley and stir until the grains glisten with the oil, about 30 seconds longer. Stir in 4½ cups (36 fl oz/1.1 l) of the broth and adjust the heat to maintain a brisk simmer. Cook the barley, stirring frequently, for about 10 minutes. Stir in the remaining 2 cups (16 fl oz/500 ml) broth, discarding the oregano sprig, and continue to simmer, stirring frequently, just until the barley is tender and creamy, about 15 minutes longer.

Meanwhile, prepare the lamb ragout: Season the lamb chunks with salt and pepper. In a frying pan over high heat, warm the olive oil. Add the lamb chunks and sauté, stirring constantly, just until they lose their pink color, 4–5 minutes. Transfer to a plate and set aside. In the same pan over medium heat, add the onions and sauté until soft, about 5 minutes. Return the lamb to the pan and stir in the tomatoes, oregano, sugar, and olives. Cook, stirring frequently, until the lamb is tender and the tomatoes are reduced to a thick sauce, about 15 minutes. Taste and adjust the seasonings with salt and pepper.

Spoon the barley risotto into warmed individual bowls. Spoon the lamb ragout on top of the risotto, garnish with the feta cheese and basil, and serve.

Serves 6

Risotto Pancakes

2 cups (10 oz/315 g) Classic Risotto
(page 7), at room temperature
1 egg, lightly beaten
2 tablespoons unsalted butter
6 tablespoons (1½ oz/45 g) grated
Parmesan cheese, plus additional
cheese for serving

*Resembling small frittatas, these pancakes make excellent use of
leftover risotto for a first course or side dish. Stir in whatever fresh
herbs that strike your fancy.*

$Place the risotto in a bowl and gently mix in the egg.

In a large nonstick frying pan over medium heat, melt
1 tablespoon of the butter. Working in batches and adding more
butter as needed to prevent sticking, drop the risotto mixture into
the pan to make 6 pancakes. Using a spatula, gently press the
risotto mixture into rounds and fry until light brown on the
bottom, about 3 minutes.

Flip the pancakes and sprinkle each one with 1 tablespoon of
the Parmesan cheese. Cover and cook until the cheese melts,
about 1 minute. Uncover and continue frying until light brown
on the bottom, about 2 minutes longer.

To serve, transfer to a warmed platter or individual plates. Pass
the additional cheese at the table.

Serves 6

Supplì with Fontina and Porcini

1 oz (30 g) dried porcini mushrooms

2 cups (16 fl oz/500 ml) hot water

2 cups (10 oz/315 g) Classic Risotto
  (*page 7*), at room temperature

2 eggs, lightly beaten

¾ cup (3 oz/90 g) fine dried bread
  crumbs

3 oz (90 g) fontina or Gouda cheese,
  cut into 12 narrow strips

vegetable oil for deep-frying

*I*n a small bowl, combine the porcini mushrooms and the hot water. Let stand for 30 minutes to soften. Using a slotted spoon, remove the mushrooms from the soaking liquid. Chop the mushrooms and place in a small saucepan. Line a sieve with cheesecloth (muslin) and pour the soaking liquid through the sieve into the small saucepan. Place the pan over medium-high heat, bring to a boil, and boil until all the liquid evaporates, about 8 minutes. Remove from the heat.

Place the risotto in a bowl. Mix in the eggs.

Line a baking sheet with waxed paper. Place the bread crumbs in a pie plate. Drop 1 tablespoon of the risotto mixture onto the bread crumbs. Using two fingers, make a slight indentation in the center of the risotto mound and place 1 cheese strip and 1 teaspoon of the porcini mixture in the indentation. Top with 1 tablespoon of the risotto mixture. Using your hands, gently form the risotto into a cylinder, with the cheese and porcini at the center. Roll in the bread crumbs to coat completely. Transfer to the lined baking sheet. Repeat to make 12 supplì in all. Cover and refrigerate for at least 1 hour or for up to 24 hours.

Preheat an oven to 250°F (120°C).

In a saucepan, pour in oil to a depth of 2 inches (5 cm). Heat to 350°F (180°C), or until a bit of bread turns golden within moments of being dropped into the oil. Working in batches, add the supplì and fry, turning occasionally to cook evenly, until golden brown, about 3 minutes. Using a slotted spoon, transfer to paper towels to drain. Then transfer to a baking sheet and keep warm in the oven while cooking the remaining supplì.

To serve, transfer the supplì to warmed individual plates.

Serves 6

Supplì with Smoked Ham and Mozzarella

3 cups (15 oz/470 g) Classic Risotto
  (page 7)
½ cup (4 fl oz/125 ml) Tomato Sauce
  (page 12)
½ cup (2 oz/60 g) grated Parmesan
  cheese
salt and ground pepper to taste
1 egg yolk, beaten
½ cup (2½ oz/75 g) fresh or thawed
  frozen English peas
1 slice smoked ham, 3 oz (90 g), cut into
  ¼-inch (6-mm) dice
3 oz (90 g) fresh or smoked mozzarella or
  Bel Paese cheese, cut into ¼-inch
  (6-mm) dice
2–3 cups (8–12 oz/250–375 g) fine dried
  bread crumbs
peanut oil or corn oil for deep-frying

To make a simple meal of these Italian supplì, serve them with warm tomato sauce and garnish with fresh basil.

❈

Prepare the Classic Risotto, omitting the yellow onion. When the rice has absorbed all the liquid and is just tender but slightly firm in the center and creamy, remove from the heat and stir in the tomato sauce and Parmesan cheese and season with salt and pepper. Let cool completely, then mix in the egg yolk.

Meanwhile, bring a small saucepan three-fourths full of water to a boil. Add the fresh or frozen peas and boil for 1 minute. Drain, immerse in cold water, and drain again. Place in a small bowl and add the ham and mozzarella or Bel Paese cheese. Toss well.

Line a baking sheet with waxed paper. Place the bread crumbs in a pie plate. Drop 1 tablespoon of the risotto mixture onto the bread crumbs. Using two fingers, make a slight indentation in the center of the risotto mound and fill with a little of the ham filling. Top with 1 tablespoon of the risotto mixture. Using your hands, gently form into a supplì the size of a large chicken egg, with the ham filling in the center. Roll in the bread crumbs to coat completely. Transfer to the lined baking sheet. Repeat to make 24 supplì in all.

Preheat an oven to 250°F (120°C).

In a saucepan, pour in oil to a depth of 3 inches (7.5 cm). Heat to 350°F (180°C), or until a bit of bread turns golden within moments of being dropped into the oil. Working in batches, add the supplì and fry, turning occasionally to cook evenly, until golden brown, 3–5 minutes. Using a slotted spoon, transfer to paper towels to drain. Then transfer to a baking sheet and keep warm in the oven while cooking the remaining supplì.

Transfer the supplì to warmed individual plates and serve.

Serves 6–8

Rosemary and Walnut Herb Croquettes

2 cups (16 fl oz/500 ml) Chicken Stock (*page 13*), Vegetable Stock (*page 12*), or broth

1 cup (7 oz/220 g) Arborio rice

⅓ cup (1½ oz/45 g) grated Parmesan cheese

1½ teaspoons finely chopped fresh rosemary, plus sprigs for garnish (optional)

⅓ cup (1½ oz/45 g) chopped walnuts

salt and ground pepper to taste

1 egg, lightly beaten

½ cup (2 oz/60 g) fine dried bread crumbs

vegetable oil or olive oil for frying

Although just as tasty and satisfying as supplì, these croquettes are a little easier to form. The recipe can be varied in many ways. Replace the rosemary with another herb or substitute pine nuts for the walnuts.

In a medium saucepan over high heat, bring the stock or broth to a boil. Add the rice and return to a boil, stirring occasionally. Reduce the heat to low, cover, and cook until the liquid is absorbed and the rice is cooked through but still sticky, about 20 minutes. Remove from the heat.

Add the Parmesan cheese, chopped rosemary, and walnuts and season with salt and pepper. Mix in the egg. Cover and refrigerate until firm enough to shape, about 2 hours.

Line a baking sheet with waxed paper. Place the bread crumbs in a pie plate. Form the rice mixture into 18 balls each 1½ inches (4 cm) in diameter. Roll them in the bread crumbs to coat evenly. Transfer to the lined baking sheet. Cover and refrigerate for at least 1 hour or up to 24 hours.

Preheat an oven to 250°F (120°C).

In a large, heavy frying pan over medium-high heat, heat enough oil to coat the bottom of the pan. Working in batches, add the croquettes and, using a spatula, flatten each until about ½ inch (12 mm) thick. Fry, turning once, until golden brown, about 2 minutes on each side. Using a spatula, transfer to paper towels to drain. Then transfer to a baking sheet and keep warm in the oven while cooking the remaining croquettes.

To serve, transfer the croquettes to warmed individual plates. Garnish with the rosemary sprigs, if using.

Serves 6

Shiitake Mushroom and Pea Risotto Pancakes

1 cup (5 oz/155 g) shelled fresh or thawed frozen English peas

3 tablespoons unsalted butter

3 oz (90 g) fresh shiitake mushrooms, brushed clean, stems removed, and coarsely chopped

2 cups (10 oz/315 g) Classic Risotto (*page 7*), at room temperature

2 tablespoons finely chopped fresh tarragon

salt and ground pepper to taste

2 eggs, lightly beaten

This is a wonderful use of any leftover risotto. Pair these delicious pancakes with a colorful mix of sautéed vegetables for a vegetarian meal. The shiitake mushrooms can be replaced with another variety.

❋

*I*f using fresh peas, bring a saucepan three-fourths full of salted water to a boil, add the peas, and cook until tender, about 8 minutes. Drain and set aside.

In a large nonstick frying pan over medium heat, melt 1 tablespoon of the butter. Add the mushrooms and sauté, tossing frequently, until they start to brown, about 3 minutes. Remove from the heat.

In a bowl, gently mix together the risotto, cooked fresh or thawed frozen peas, sautéed mushrooms, and tarragon. Season with salt and pepper, then gently mix in the eggs.

Return the same frying pan to medium heat and melt 1 table-spoon of the butter. Working in batches and adding more butter as needed to prevent sticking, drop the risotto mixture into the pan to make 12 small pancakes. Using a spatula, gently press the risotto mixture into rounds. Fry the pancakes, turning once, until lightly browned, about 4 minutes on each side.

To serve, transfer to warmed individual plates.

Serves 4

Supplì with Mozzarella and Fresh Herbs

2 cups (16 fl oz/500 ml) water
salt to taste
1 cup (7 oz/220 g) Arborio rice
2 eggs, lightly beaten
5 tablespoons (1¼ oz/37 g) grated
    Parmesan cheese
ground pepper to taste
ground nutmeg to taste
¾ cup (3 oz/90 g) fine dried bread
    crumbs
1 tablespoon chopped fresh marjoram
    or sage
½ lb (250 g) mozzarella cheese, cut into
    12–16 small cubes
peanut oil for deep-frying

In a saucepan, bring the water to a boil, season lightly with salt, and stir in the rice. Reduce the heat to low, cover, and cook until the water has been absorbed and the rice is cooked through but still sticky, about 20 minutes.

Meanwhile, oil a rimmed baking sheet. When the rice is ready, remove from the heat and mix in the eggs and Parmesan cheese. Season with salt, pepper, and nutmeg. Spread the rice evenly on the prepared baking sheet, cover, and let cool in the refrigerator.

Line a baking sheet with waxed paper. Place the bread crumbs in a pie plate. Spread the chopped herb in another pie plate and roll the cheese cubes in the chopped herb. Drop a heaping tablespoonful of the risotto mixture onto the bread crumbs. Using two fingers, make a slight indentation in the center of the risotto mound and tuck a piece of mozzarella into the indentation. Using your hands, gently smooth the rice over the cheese. Finish shaping the rice to make a supplì 1½ inches (4 cm) in diameter. Roll in the bread crumbs to coat completely. Transfer to the lined baking sheet. Repeat to make 12–16 supplì in all.

Preheat an oven to 250°F (120°C).

In a saucepan, pour oil to a depth of 3 inches (7.5 cm). Heat to 350°F (180°C), or until a bit of bread turns golden within moments of being dropped into the oil. Working in batches, add the supplì and fry, turning occasionally to cook evenly, until golden brown, 3–5 minutes. Using a slotted spoon, transfer to paper towels to drain. Then transfer to a baking sheet and keep warm in the oven (for no more than 10 minutes) while cooking the remaining supplì.

Transfer the supplì to a warmed platter and serve.

Serves 4–6

Glossary

The following glossary defines terms both generally and as they relate specifically to preparing risotto, including major and unusual ingredients and basic techniques.

ARTICHOKES
These flower buds of a type of thistle native to the Mediterranean have, at their center, a tender, gray-green base topped by a prickly, inedible choke, enclosed by a cluster of tough, pointed leaves. Artichokes are added to risotto after their stems and outer leaves are trimmed and their chokes are removed. Baby artichokes need only light trimming of their outer leaves before they are cooked.

ARUGULA
Green leaf vegetable with slender, multiple-lobed leaves that are chopped and added to risotto to impart a peppery, slightly bitter flavor. Also known as rocket.

ASPARAGUS
Member of the lily family that produces long, slender stalks with a compact bud at one end. The tender tips are especially prized for use in risottos and other savory dishes.

The most common variety is green; white spears are occasionally available in well-stocked markets and greengrocers.

BALSAMIC VINEGAR
A specialty of Modena, Italy, balsamic vinegar is made from reduced grape juice and is aged many years to give it a sweet, pungent flavor.

BEETS
Root vegetable with a round bulb and long, dark green stalks and leaves. The most common variety is a deep purplish red; other varieties have yellowish orange, orange, or white-and-red flesh. Both the bulb, which is slightly sweet when cooked, and the greens, which have a sturdy texture, are edible.

BREAD CRUMBS, DRIED
Dried bread crumbs add body to shaped risottos and are used to coat such specialties as supplì and croquettes before they are fried.

To make dried crumbs, choose a good-quality coarse country bread made of unbleached wheat flour, with a firm, coarse-textured crumb. Cut away the crusts and crumble the bread by hand or in a blender or a food processor. Spread the crumbs on a baking sheet, place in an oven set at its lowest temperature, and dry slowly, about 1 hour. Store in a covered container at room temperature. Dried bread crumbs, usually fine textured, are also sold prepackaged in food stores.

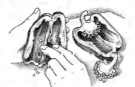

BROCCOLI
Related to cabbage, this popular green cruciferous vegetable is used in many rice dishes in the form of its small flowering buds, called florets. When cutting florets from broccoli stalks, include about 1 inch (2.5 cm) of the stem with each floret.

BUTTERNUT SQUASH
A pale, yellowish tan winter squash with yellow to orange flesh. Commonly 8–12 inches (20–30 cm) long, it has a broad, bulblike base and an elongated neck. In season from early autumn through winter.

CAPERS
These small, pickled buds of a bush common to the Mediterranean are pickled in salt and vinegar and used whole or chopped as a savory flavoring or garnish.

BELL PEPPERS
Bell-shaped members of the pepper family whose sweet flesh is a welcome addition to risotto. They are commonly sold in the unripe green form; ripened red or yellow varieties are also available. Also known as capsicums.

To prepare raw bell peppers, cut each pepper in half lengthwise with a sharp knife. Pull out the stem section from each half, along with the cluster of seeds attached to it. Remove any remaining seeds, along with any thin white membranes, or ribs, to which they are attached. Cut as directed in specific recipes.

To roast bell peppers, preheat a broiler (griller). After seeding the peppers, place the halves, cut side down, on a baking sheet and broil until the skins blacken and blister. Remove from the broiler, drape loosely with aluminum foil, and let stand until the peppers soften and are cool enough to handle, about 10 minutes. Using your fingertips or a small knife, peel off the blackened skins. Then tear or cut as directed in the recipe.

CLAM JUICE
The strained liquid of shucked clams, sold in small bottles in the fresh or canned seafood departments of food stores. Because of its refreshing briny flavor, the juice is used as an alternative to homemade fish stock for cooking risottos that feature seafood.

EGGPLANTS
Mildly earthy, sweet vegetable-fruits with creamy white flesh and tough, shiny skin. The skin varies in color from purple, the most commonly seen variety, to green to red to white, and may be peeled or left intact in long-cooked dishes such as risotto. Also available is the slender, purple Asian eggplant (below), which has more tender flesh and fewer, smaller seeds. Also known as aubergine.

ENGLISH PEAS
These shelled peas, also called green peas, have a sweet flavor and tender texture appreciated in risotto. When purchasing fresh peas, choose pods that are plump and bright green. Peas are also available frozen; the small variety sometimes labeled "petite peas" or "petite pois" is an acceptable substitute for fresh peas.

ESCAROLE
This variety of chicory has broad, curly, bright green leaves and a refreshingly bitter

flavor. Like other greens, escarole is sliced or shredded and added to risotto for its texture as well as its color and flavor. Also known as Batavian endive.

FENNEL
Bulb vegetable with a crisp, refreshing, mildly anise flavor. Before using in recipes, the stems and feathery tops and any bruised outer stalks are cut off the bulb. The bulb is then thinly sliced and added to risotto, and the fine, feathery leaves are used fresh as an herb garnish.

GARLIC
Pungent bulb popular worldwide as a flavoring ingredient, both raw and cooked. For the best flavor, purchase whole heads of dry garlic and separate individual cloves from the head as needed.

To peel a garlic clove, place on a work surface and cover with the side of a large chef's knife. Press down firmly on the side of the knife to crush the clove slightly; the dry skin will then slip off easily.

GINGER
The knobby rhizome of the tropical ginger plant. Whole ginger rhizomes, commonly but mistakenly called roots, are usually purchased fresh and are peeled before use in recipes.

KALE
This member of the cabbage family has long, crinkly, dark green leaves that are sliced and added to risotto for their strong flavor and sturdy texture.

LEEKS
Long, cylindrical member of the onion family with a pale white root end, dark green leaves, and moderate flavor. Grown in sandy soil, leeks must be thoroughly cleaned before use.

To clean leeks, trim off the roots. Trim off the dark green leaves where they meet the pale green part of the stem. Starting about 1 inch (2.5 cm) from the root end, slit each leek lengthwise. Vigorously swish each leek

in a basin or sink filled with cold water. Drain and rinse again; check to make sure that no dirt remains between the tightly packed pale portion of the leaves.

MARSALA
Amber Italian wine, dry or sweet in flavor, from the area of Marsala, in Sicily.

MUSHROOMS
The meaty texture and rich flavor of mushrooms complement many risotto dishes.

Cremini These cultivated mushrooms have brown caps and white stems. Although they resemble cultivated white mushrooms, cremini are often more flavorful.

Cultivated White Common variety with white caps and white stems, readily available in food stores and greengrocers. The smallest white mushrooms, with their caps still closed, are known as button mushrooms.

Porcini Pale brown mushrooms sometimes available fresh but often used in their dried form. Before use, dried porcini are softened in hot water for 30 minutes.

Portobello Mature form of the cremini mushroom. The large, dark brown caps, 4–6 inches (10–15 cm) in diameter, have a particularly robust texture.

Shiitake Meaty-flavored Asian mushrooms with flat, dark brown caps usually 2–3 inches (5–7.5 cm) in diameter. They are sold fresh in Asian markets and well-stocked food stores.

NUTS
An array of nuts are used to add crisp, crunchy texture to risottos. Almonds, oval in shape, have a mellow, sweet flavor. They are sold whole (with their skins intact), blanched (with their skins removed), slivered, or thinly sliced (flaked). Walnuts are rich, crisp nuts with distinctively crinkled surfaces. Hazelnuts, which are spherical in shape, are slightly sweet; they are

also known as filberts. Pine nuts are the small, ivory seeds from the cones of a species of pine tree. They possess a rich, subtly resinous flavor.

OILS

Not only do oils provide a medium in which foods may be browned without sticking, but they also subtly enhance the flavor of many dishes. Of the several varieties of olive oils produced, extra virgin is the most flavorful. Extracted from olives on the first pressing without use of heat or chemicals, it is prized for its pure, fruity taste and golden to pale green hue. Products labeled "pure olive oil" are milder in aroma and flavor and may be used for all-purpose cooking. Pale gold peanut oil has a subtle hint of the peanut's richness. Asian sesame oil is made with toasted sesame seeds, resulting in a dark, strong oil used primarily as a flavoring. Vegetable and seed oils, such as safflower, canola, and corn oil, are employed for their high cooking temperatures and bland flavor.

OLIVES, KALAMATA

These black, or ripe, olives, cured in brine and packed in vinegar, are used in many Mediterranean-style dishes.

Look for Greek Kalamata olives sold in jars in well-stocked food stores or in bulk in delicatessens.

ONIONS

A range of onions is used to add their mild and sweet or strong and pungent flavors to meat, poultry, seafood, and vegetable risotto dishes.

Green Also called spring onion or scallion, the green onion is harvested immature, including leaves, before the bulb has formed. Both green and white parts are enjoyed for their mild but still pronounced onion flavor.

Red This mild, sweet onion has purplish red skin and red-tinged white flesh. Also known as Spanish onion.

Yellow Distinguished by its dry, yellowish brown skin, this popular onion has strong-flavored white flesh.

PANCETTA

Unsmoked bacon that has been cured simply with salt and pepper and is chopped or diced before adding to risotto dishes. Available in Italian delicatessens and well-stocked food stores, it is sold flat or is sliced from a large sausage-shaped roll.

PROSCIUTTO

This raw ham, a specialty of Parma, Italy, is cured by dry-salting for 1 month, then air-drying in cool curing sheds for 6 months or longer. Chopped or diced prosciutto contributes deep pink color and distinctive

intense flavor to risotto. It is added toward the end of cooking to preserve its tender texture. Look for prosciutto in Italian delicatessens and well-stocked food stores.

RADICCHIO

Spherical variety of chicory whose most common type has small reddish purple leaves with pronounced white ribs. Other varieties are slightly tapered and vary in color. Thinly sliced radicchio adds an appealing bitter flavor and subtle texture to risotto.

RED PEPPER FLAKES

Spice consisting of coarsely ground flakes of dried red chiles, including the seeds, which add moderately hot flavor to risottos and other savory dishes.

SAFFRON

Intensely aromatic, golden orange spice made from the dried stigmas of a species of crocus and used to perfume and color many classic Mediterranean dishes, including risotto and other rice dishes. Sold either as threads—the dried stigmas—or in powdered form. For the best quality, look for products labeled "pure saffron."

SHALLOT

Small member of the onion family with brownish skin, white flesh

tinged with purple, and a flavor resembling a cross between sweet onion and garlic.

SPINACH

This assertive-tasting vegetable has smooth or crinkly green leaves that vary in size. Small-leaved spinach is more delicate in flavor. Spinach leaves must be rinsed thoroughly to eliminate all dirt and sand.

To clean spinach, place the leaves in a sink or large basin and fill with cold water to cover generously. Agitate the leaves in the water to remove the dirt, then lift the leaves out of the water and set aside. Drain the sink or basin, rinsing well. Repeat the procedure until no grit remains.

SWISS CHARD

Leafy, dark green vegetable with thick, crisp white or red stems and ribs. The green part, often trimmed from the stems and ribs, is cooked like spinach and has a milder flavor.

TOMATOES, DRIED

When sliced crosswise or halved, then dried in the sun, tomatoes develop an intense, sweet-tart flavor and a pleasantly chewy texture that enhance savory recipes such as risotto. Sun-dried tomatoes are available packed in oil or dry in specialty-food shops and well-stocked markets.

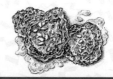

SHELLFISH
Nearly all varieties of shellfish can be incorporated into or served alongside risotto. Purchase fresh shellfish that are free of off odors and smell only of the clean scent of the sea. Avoid any bivalve mollusks that gape open.

Clams Bivalve mollusks valued for their sweet, tender flesh. Clams are sold live in their shells or sometimes already shucked. Before cooking clams, scrub them under cold running water with a small, stiff-bristled brush and discard any whose shells do not close tightly to the touch.

Crabs These crustaceans found in salt or fresh water yield succulent white meat available fresh, frozen, or canned. For the best flavor, seek out fresh crabmeat or purchase already steamed or boiled whole crabs from a fish market. Request that the crabs be cracked, which facilitates extracting the meat from the shells.

Lobsters Large crustaceans with firm, white flesh. Already cooked, cleaned, and shelled lobster meat is available in some fish markets, but for the best results, purchase live lobsters and cook according to the directions in recipes.

Sea Scallops Large variety (below, right) of the bivalve mollusk with rounds of flesh about 1½ inches (4 cm) in diameter. Scallops are usually sold already shelled but may sometimes be found in their shell complete with their sweet-flavored, orange-pink corals attached. Bay scallops (above, left) are much smaller, measuring about ½ inch (12 mm) in diameter.

Shrimp Crustaceans with firm, delectable flesh. Raw shrimp (prawns) are generally sold with the heads already removed but the shells still intact. Before cooking, they are usually peeled and their veinlike intestinal tracts removed.

To peel and devein shrimp, using your thumbs, split open the shrimp's thin shell along the concave side, between its two rows of legs. Peel away the shell, taking care to leave the last segment with the tail fin intact and attached to the meat if specified in the recipe. Using a small, sharp knife, make a shallow slit along the back of the shrimp just deep enough to expose the long, usually dark-

colored veinlike intestinal tract. With the tip of the knife or a finger, lift up and pull out the vein, then discard.

TOMATOES, FRESH
When tomatoes are in season, use the best sun-ripened tomatoes available. At other times of the year, plum tomatoes, sometimes call Roma or egg tomatoes (below), are likely to have the best flavor and texture. For cooking, canned whole, diced, or chopped plum tomatoes are a good substitute.

To peel tomatoes, bring a saucepan of water to a boil. Using a small, sharp knife, cut out the core from the stem end of each tomato, then cut a shallow X in the skin at the tomato's base. Submerge for about 20 seconds in the boiling water, then

remove and cool in a bowl of cold water. Starting at the X, peel the skin from the tomato, using your fingertips and, if necessary, the knife blade.

To seed tomatoes, cut each in half crosswise. Squeeze gently to force out the seed sacs.

ZEST
Thin, brightly colored, outermost layer of a lemon, orange, or other citrus fruit. This lively source of flavor containing the fruit's essential oils is added to risottos and other savory dishes, as well as sweet preparations.

To remove zest in very thin strips, use a simple tool known as a zester, drawing its sharp-edged holes across the skin of a

fruit. The fine holes on a hand-held grater can also be used.

To remove zest in wider strips, hold the edge of a paring knife or vegetable peeler almost parallel to the fruit's skin and carefully cut off the zest. Take care not to remove any bitter white pith with it. The strips can then be cut with a knife into narrow pieces.

ZUCCHINI
Slender and tube shaped, this variety of squash has edible green, yellow, or green-and-cream-striped skin and pale, tender flesh. Also known as summer squash or courgette. Look for smaller-sized squashes, which have a finer texture and flavor.

Index

ACKNOWLEDGMENTS

The following authors provided the recipes for this book:
Kristine Kidd: pages 15, 21, 22, 25, 26, 30, 33, 35, 36, 39, 52, 55, 73, 76, 78, 81, 84, 89, 93, 94, 99, 100;
Norman Kolpas: pages 16, 40, 45, 56, 59, 60, 62, 65, 66, 70, 75, 82, 87, 90; Joanne Weir: pages 18, 42, 50, 96;
Chuck Williams: page 29, 49; Joyce Goldstein: page 69, 102; John Phillip Carroll: page 46.

The publishers thank the following people for their generous assistance and support in producing this book:
Desne Border, Ken DellaPenta, Julia Schlosser, Heidi Gintner, Susan Massey, and Kim Konecny.
The following kindy lent props for the photography: Sue Fisher King, Williams-Sonoma, Pottery Barn,
Birodi Art Imports, and Fillamento. The publishers also thank all the other individuals and organizations
that provided props, locations, and other assistance in producing this book.

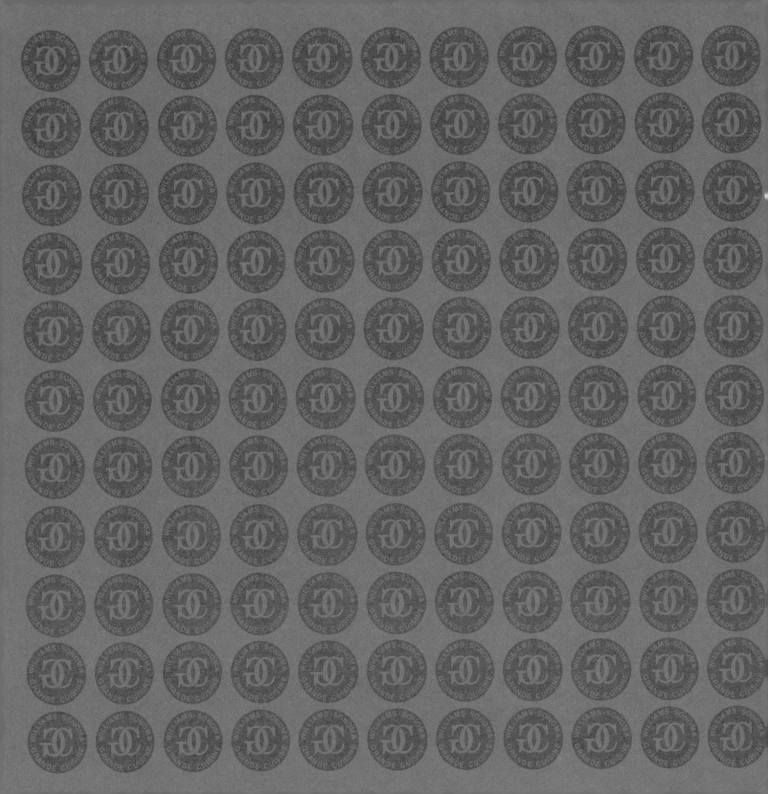